GRACIA & GENTIL: Hymn Stories For Our Contemporary Lifestyles

MUGERWA Paul
MBA-Investment Management;
School of Business and Computing
Bugema University, Uganda
CEO, Asante Capital Hub Ltd
Kampala, Uganda
(Financial Services, Tax & Business Consultancy)

Church Elder & Practicing Musician
E-mail: tatagracia2007@gmail.com

Devotional, Inspirational and Historical Book for everyone.

GRACIA & GENTIL:
Hymn Stories For Our Contemporary Lifestyles

Copyright @ 2015 EPS Publishers Ltd

P.O Box 33877 Kampala

All Rights Reserved.

ISBN: 978-9970-565-01-6

Concept Editor: Dr. Ikechukwu Michael Oluikpe

Production Editor: Prof. Reuben T. Mugerwa

Sole Contributor: Mugerwa Paul, P.O Box 36750 Kampala

0782640448   Email: tatagracia2007@gmail.com

Layout Design: Wakabi Joe

Cover page Design: Ssenono Emmanuel (Corporate Impression Agency)

Content: Music / Church Hymns, Personal Development, Spiritual, Inspirational, Christian Historical Context, Theology.

No part of this publication may be reproduced or distributed in any form or by any media, or stored in a database or retrieval system without the prior written permission of the author or publisher.

DETAILED TABLE OF CONTENTS

FOREWORD …………………………………………..	| 13
ACKNOWLEDGEMENTS ……………………………….	| 16
EDITORIAL TEAM ………………………………………	| 17
DEDICATION …………………………………………..	| 17
PREFACE ……………………………………………….	| 18
GENERAL BACKGROUND TO THE BOOK …………….	| 20
MARRYING THEORY & PRACTICE ……………………	| 21
LAY-OUT OF THE TEXTS (SONGS) ……………………	| 24
1. O WORSHIP THE KING ……………………………	| 26
2. O GOD, OUR HELP IN AGES PAST ………………	| 29
3. JESUS SHALL REIGN WHERE'VER THE SUN ………	| 32
4. THERE IS POWER IN THE BLOOD …………………	| 35
5. TELL ME THE STORY OF JESUS ……………………	| 37
6. TAKE THE NAME OF JESUS WITH YOU ………….	| 39
7. AMAZING GRACE ……………………………….	| 43
8. HOW SWEET THE NAME OF JESUS SOUNDS: ……	| 45
9. OPEN MY EYES …………………………………….	| 50
10. BECAUSE HE LIVES ……………………………….	| 53
11. I SING THE ALMIGHTY POWER OF GOD ……….	| 58

12. LORD, I HEAR OF SHOWERS OF
    BLESSINGS (EVEN ME) .... | 62
13. WHAT A DAY THAT WILL BE .... | 66
14. SWEETER AS THE YEARS GO BY .... | 68
15. IN MY HEART THERE RINGS A MELODY .... | 71
16. STANDING ON THE PROMISES .... | 73
17. SINCE JESUS CAME INTO MY HEART .... | 76
18. I LOVE TO TELL THE STORY .... | 79
19. TELL ME THE OLD OLD STORY .... | 82
20. HE LEADETH ME .... | 86
21. IS MY NAME WRITTEN THERE?? .... | 88
22. WE HAVE HEARD A JOYFUL SOUND,
    JESUS SAVES! .... | 90
23. GOD BE WITH YOU TILL WE MEET AGAIN .... | 93
24. TIS LOVE THAT MAKES US HAPPY .... | 95
25. GOD WILL TAKE CARE OF YOU .... | 99
26. I SHALL KNOW HIM (WHEN MY LIFE
    WORK IS ENDED) .... | 102
27. WE KNOW NOT THE HOUR .... | 105
28. STAND UP FOR JESUS .... | 108
29. LOVE DIVINE, ALL LOVES EXCELLING .... | 112

30. HOW GREAT THOU ART	| 115
31. THE OLD RUGGED CROSS	| 118
32. RESCUE THE PERISHING	| 121
33. COME THOU FOUNT OF EVERY BLESSING	| 123
34. NEAR TO THE HEART OF GOD	| 126
35. HOW FIRM A FOUNDATION	| 128
36. O HAPPY DAY	| 132
37. PEACE, BE STILL	| 135
38. ALL THE WAY MY SAVIOR LEADS ME	| 138
39. IT IS WELL WITH MY SOUL	| 141
40. PRAISE GOD FROM WHOM ALL BLESSINGS FLOW	| 144
41. I SURRENDER ALL	| 147
42. NEARER MY GOD TO THEE	| 150
42. WERE YOU THERE??	| 152
43. MORE ABOUT JESUS	| 155
45. 'TIS SO SWEET TO TRUST IN JESUS	| 158
46. I MUST TELL JESUS	| 161
47. ROCK OF AGES, CLEFT FOR ME	| 163
48. WHAT A FRIEND WE HAVE IN JESUS	| 166

49. HE LIVES, (I SERVE A RISEN SAVIOUR) .... | 169

50. I GAVE MY LIFE FOR THEE .... | 172

51. HOLY, HOLY, HOLY! LORD GOD ALMIGHTY .... | 175

52. JESUS, KEEP ME NEAR THE CROSS .... | 179

53. MY JESUS, I LOVE THEE .... | 183

54. A MIGHTY FORTRESS IS OUR GOD .... | 185

55. BRINGING IN THE SHEAVES
(SOWING IN THE MORNING) .... | 190

56. JUST AS I AM .... | 194

57. LORD, I'M COMING HOME .... | 197

58. CHIEF OF SINNERS THOUGH I BE .... | 200

59. THE MESSIAH .... | 202

60. BENEATH THE CROSS OF JESUS .... | 206

BIBLIOGRAPHY & REFERENCE SECTION .... | 210

"Reading Scriptures ignite in us interest to know more about God's promises for His people. Singing Scripture is a call to worship which brings about transformation. A new song is about one's testimony of God's goodness. Reading through this well articulated and assembled book will help you to appreciate God's love, His faithfulness, and open your heart to worship Him in spirit and in truth, John 4:24."

SIMON PETER MUKHAMA, GENERAL SECRETARY/ CEO

THE BIBLE SOCIETY OF UGANDA

"This book has the potential to inspire and cause a revival of genuine worship through meaningful music in the Christian church. Reflecting the spiritual lessons in these well-known Christian hymns and gospel songs will result in an experience of worship on a deeper level through singing with the mind and the spirit.

I recommend this book as a must-read for those who seek to experience more meaningful Christian worship through singing the gospel."

IKECHUKWU MICHAEL OLUIKPE, PHD

(BIBLICAL STUDIES- NEW TESTAMENT),

LECTURER, SCHOOL OF THEOLOGY AND RELIGIOUS STUDIES,

BUGEMA UNIVERSITY, UGANDA

Often times, when we open our song and hymn books to sing in churches, at homes and other gatherings, we have no idea that the lyric and music have a deep emotional and spiritual background. Mr. Mugerwa has joined a few of those who prove us wrong. He has rewound the events to reveal to us that these pieces evolved from real human experience with life and with their God. Sending us to such scenarios inspires us to envision a character behind a song and have a personal touch with the experience of the composer, sharing with him/her the awesome spiritual and passionate aura.

Additionally, the divide between us and the composers is so vast that we may not get to grips with their feelings and inspiration. Singing A shelter in the time of storm without experiential knowledge that a rock is the surest life safety when a devastating storm hits; it is singing without the real touch on the matter. Mugerwa helps us to touch different and varying historical, sociological, geographical and spiritual backdrops that inspired the songs and hymns. He makes us appreciate the songs and hymns much more. I strongly commend his work and recommend that we browse through information to have a profounder worshipping experience.

BWAMBALE SIMON, PhD (Theology & Ministry)

Director, Bugema University – Kampala Campus

This book clearly shows that, if all the aspects of a context are carefully kept in mind ,when interpreting music, a much more accurate knowledge of its truth will be known. A faithful adherence to situation will create in the interpreter an honest appreciation of the song. As we understand the circumstances that occasioned the authors composition, we are deterred from attaching ideas to his writing that are completely foreign to the purpose of the song. The take in this book is the most important tool to understanding the original purpose to the hymns in this book. Gracia & Gentil: Hymns stories for Our Contemporary Lifestyles, gives readers a tremendous platform for helping to learn to sing with a purpose and reflect our lives. We congratulate the author of this book upon this outstanding achievement.

STEPHEN KABUYE, Mayor Emeritus (Entebbe Municipality)

President Lake Victoria Regional Local Authority Cooperation; and Vice President Local Authority Confronting Disaster and Emergencies

This is a very exciting and wonderful compilation of historical background of the most common Christian hymn in a single book. The book helps the reader to get deeper meaning of the hymn after knowing the circumstances surrounding its composition. We must thank Mr. Mugerwa for researching and sharing with us the richness of Christian music tradition. The rich testimonies shared in this book will certainly make singing these hymns very enjoyable and meaningful. I have no doubt that so many souls will be touched as a result of worshipping using this book. I highly recommend it to all God loving families, fellowships and church congregations.

KIYINGI ELIJAH, UNIVERSITY SECRETARY

NDEJJE UNIVERSITY

(AN ANGLICAN CHURCH INSTITUTION IN UGANDA)

The Hebrew Psalter constitutes one of the largest and most complex hymns in human history. Its proportionate size in comparison with the rest of Hebrew literature is a clear testimony to the perpetual value and emphasis the Hebrews attached to their worship and praise. That music is part of worship is clearly attested in the book of Psalms being the most voluminous and most comprehensive in the entire Bible. As Christians, we do well to discover the true import of the intertwining fabric of praise and worship in our relationship with God. In our joys and sorrows; in our perplexities and delights, doubts and successes, apparent disappointments and glowing experiences, we would pick a leaf from the Israelites by composing or singing a song about our experiences with God.

The selection of the songs in this book constitutes those songs which were not only borne out of common human experiences, but also of outstanding, all-time musical composition. They have spoken to various people throughout the ages and under various circumstances. Without any shadow of doubt, I believe these songs will continue to appeal to many more people from all walks of life and under varied circumstances they find themselves in. I recommend this book to all worshippers of God and all lovers of music.

MOSES MAKA NDIMUKIKA, PhD

PROFESSOR OF THE OLD TESTAMENT EXEGESIS AND THEOLOGY

"……..who thought up the fantastic hymns we all enjoy? ….so many of us ask ourselves. Mugerwa Paul has started a journey that will no doubt bless every reader with straight answers to a long standing dilemma! The amount of research he has put into the historical aspect of these carefully selected hymns deserves everyone's attention. Have a blessed reading!

ELDER KASOZI GIDEON, POPULAR CHURCH MUSIC TRAINER & PRODUCER

IN THE EAST AFRICA COMMUNITY.

One of the most effective ways known for fixing God's word in our memory is through repeating them in song. Such song has wonderful power. Such power subdues rude and uncultivated natures, quickens thoughts and awakens sympathy according to Ellen G. White in her book The Voice in Speech and Song (VSS 407,2). This simple book Gracia & Gentil: Hymn Stories, is another dimension to all these; It opens to us themes behind these hymns so we can sing with Empathy, sharing the experiences and thoughts of the authors which no doubt enhances our understanding and appreciation of why we chose one song and may be not another for a certain occasion. It is presented in an easy to read style, how I wish and pray we could always acquaint ourselves with these stories behind our loved Hymns!

SOLOMON W. MANGENI (MIEEE,MIET),

PHD STUDENT-ADVANCED TELECOMMUNICATIONS AND

BUSINESS DEVELOPMENT; SWANSEA UNIVERSITY - WALES, UK

This book is a must read for anyone looking for fresh and contemporary Christian message from the hymns used in today's worship. Paul writes from a very personal point of view which helps one relate to the experiences he talks about easily. To the reader, this book represents grounded faith whose conviction inspires devotion and worship in every Christian of today. These timeless hymns come alive and help one to understand God and relate Him to real life experiences easily helping one derive purpose for which we have been created.

ELDER (ENG.) MUWONGE JONATHAN

This book helps the reader to understand the meaning of a song, the circumstances in which the song was written and the purpose of the song other than the rhythm of the song itself. The meaning of a song can vary drastically from person to person. This book reveals that other purpose at work. When you bring a song out of context, conclusions made by the said song may be different than if the context was used in perspective. It goes on to describe the historical context of the songs. Understanding the perspective of a song is critical to our congregational singing today. Reading this book arms you with the background that can be useful in helping you receive and give advice in our contemporary lives. It is a tool not only to reveal the circumstances that occasioned the composition of a certain song but also helps us meet a stranger experiencing the same situation like we face in our daily lives.

ROSETTE KABUYE, PhD (SOCIAL POLICY)

Mugerwa Paul's publication has the capacity to enliven our congregational singing, to rekindle a dying and desperate Christian soul, and reawaken Christians across da board toward a renewed relationship with God, the initiator of music and worship. Studying this text will reward any reader with an appreciative conception of the love, grace, triumph and leadership of our loving God in our contemporary lives. It is a must read for any mortal being in this painful world.

ELDER (ENG.) KAWOOYA ABRAHAM BYANDALA, HEAD ELDER- SDA CHURCH NAJJANANKUMBI DISTRICT COUNCIL

While many authors have written about the historical context of hymns, it is hard to find a compilation of all into one document. In addition, not many have used the historical context and applied it to our contemporary lifestyles, as Mr. Mugerwa Paul has done. It is this gap that this book is addressing, and so I recommend it to all Christian as a must-read.

ELD. GILBERT KAMANGA,

NATIONAL DIRECTOR — WORLD VISION UGANDA

FOREWORD

It is always presumptuous for humans to try to say anything significant about God—even in hymns and songs of praise. When God acted decisively in history in order to save Israel, she did not keep silent; not only did Israel repeatedly take up her pen to recall these acts of God to her mind in historical documents, but she also addressed Yahweh in a wholly personal way. Israel offered praise to Him, and asked Him questions, and complained to Him about all her sufferings, for Yahweh had not chosen His people as a mere dumb object of His will in history, but to commune with Him and this is what the most part of the Psalter does. Ceaseless was the praise which Israel offered up to their God which could be categorized in different titles as we shall see here below. Christians have inherited the Hebrew culture of responding to our God, in hymns and songs, for the goodness He has done for us.

The Hebrew Psalter was by no means an isolated literary phenomenon but a posture of intensely religious activities as reflected in their attitudes in a wide variety of extant literature which included epic poetry, hymns, penitential psalms, prayers, incantations, thanksgivings, and petitions addressed to Yahweh. Putting it differently, the Psalms of the Hebrews must be considered suigeneris since they constituted the supreme example of religious devotion and served as effective vehicle for the propagation of truths unfolded in the process of divine revelation.

Take this book for what it is, a commentary on a compilation of several confessions of different individuals at different times in history who, like the Hebrews of the old, took poetry and grouped it in order to form stanzas and strophes turned them into a beautiful melody as an expression of their faith.

As it was in the Psalter, hymns and songs were never written by one person. Allusions to authorship most frequently embrace the seventy-three compositions attributed to David. However others were also mentioned like Solomon with two titles (Ps. 72 and 127) and one psalm was attributed to Moses (Ps. 90). Mention of literary types within the psalm titles include the common description "song" (shir), occurring in some thirty instances, and frequently associated with mizmor, which is found in fifty-seven titles. Other varieties include a psalm for the Sabbath (Ps 92), one used at the dedication of the Temple, a wedding song (Ps. 45), an instructional composition (Ps. 60), a psalm of "testimony" (Ps. 80), a psalm of praise (Ps. 145) and many others.

Musical instruments, as we use them today to accompany our singing so it was also in the Hebrew Psalter. The musical instruments were referred to under the names Nehiloth (Ps. 5), which occurs only here in the Old Testament and is consequently obscure in meaning, and Sheminith (Pss. 6, 12), but the latter seems to refer to an "octave", and in its only other occurrence (1 Chron. 15:21) it is of a doubtful meaning. Stringed instruments as such are mentioned in the titles of Psalms 4, 6, 54, 55, 67 and 76. Four of these also contain the word mizmor pointing clearly to instrumental accompaniment of singers.

As it is today, so it was in those days that individuals or guilds of singers appeared under various designations, one of the more common being Asaph (Pss. 50, 78-83); a prominent court-musician in the time of David and the monarchy. Ugaritic sources have testified very well to the existence of a class of Temple personnel known assarim, who were analogous to the Hebrew singers of the monarchy and later times. As far as the Psalter is concerned, Asaph could refer either to the guild, to some member of it, or to their collection of religious poetry. The mention of Ethan the Ezrahite (Ps. 89; cf, 1 Chron. 6:44; in 1

Kings 4:31 Ethan is a Hebrew sage. There is another one by the name of Heman the Ezrahite (Ps. 88; cf 1 Chron. 6:33) enshrined the native Canaanite tradition of music and psalmody. The mention of the sons of Korah (Pss. 42, 44-49, 84-85, 87-88) may imply the existence of another musical guild whose tradition origins probably reached back to Korah, the great-grandson of Levi (Num. 16:1ff; 1 Chron. 6:31ff.; 2 Chron. 20:19).

Finally, the Bible says that Praise God with shouts of joy, all people! Sing to the glory of his name; offer him glorious praise (66:1-2). Elsewhere, Sing a new song to the Lord; praise him in the assembly of his faithful people (149:1)! This book is just about that. Let us do just that in our Christian experience for ever more,

PROF. REUBEN T. MUGERWA, DVC – ACADEMICS & PROFESSOR OF

BIBLICAL THEOLOGY

BUGEMA UNIVERSITY, 2015.

ACKNOWLEDGEMENTS

Despite the efforts of a couple of people (theologians, academicians, musicians, church leaders and members), in a unique book of this size that is not only a devotional, inspirational but also a historical, errors can't be avoided. Any error you come across is the responsibility of Mugerwa Paul. Certainly, errors are not the responsibility of the excellent people at EPS Publishers Ltd & other technicians who have helped us. These include the resourceful Mr. Mayanja Ali, Mr. Wakabi Joe, and Mr. Ssenono Emmanuel, in the lay-out, concept and cover page designing ; musical theoretical advisors Mr. Sseruyange David, Mr. Ssaabwe Moses, Eld. Kasozi Gideon, Pastor Nyanzi; and Mrs. Rebecca Nakisozi Mugerwa, Co-author and whose fixes and suggestions make the book more readable than it otherwise would have been; and my parents (Mr & Mrs. Paul & Ritah Ssali). My dear brothers and sisters, plus Muko Ssekandi William have furnished me with all spiritual, moral, financial and intellectual support to complete this publication.

Frankly, I was fortunate to have the following Reviewers of this book, whose advice was invaluable:

Prof. Reuben T. Mugerwa, DVC – Academics: Bugema University.

Mr. Mukhama Simon Peter, GS/ CEO: The Bible Society of Uganda.

Dr. Kafeero M. Israel, Executive Secretary: Uganda Union of the SDA Church.

Dr. Bwambale Simon, Director- Kampala Campus: Bugema University.

Dr. Ikechukwu Michael Oluikpe, Lecturer- Sch. Of Theology: Bugema University.

Mr. Kiyingi Elijah, University Secretary: Ndejje University.

Mr. Kamanga Gilbert, National Director: World Vision Uganda.

Eld. Kabuye Stephen, Head Elder SDA Church Najjanankumbi & Mayor Emeritus.

Dr. Moses Maka Ndimukika, Professor of Exegesis & Theology.

Eld. (Eng.)Kawooya Abraham, Head Elder – SDA Church Najjanankumbi District.

Eld. Jonathan Muwonge.

Eld. (Eng.) Mangeni Solomon, Swansea University – UK

Dr. Rosette Kabuye, University of Kent - UK

Editorial Team

Dr. Lukwago Moses (Phd – Makerere University)

Dr. Ikechukwu Michael Oluikpe (PhD Biblical Studies- New Testament)

DEDICATION

This publication is dedicated to:
My lovely children- Namuli Gracia Ritah and Katumba Gentil Reuben
My gorgeous nieces- Nanyunja Jeyvon, Jasmine, Erica, Abigael
My beloved nephews- Baatte , Ethan, Xavier, Darius, Moses, Dalisto.
Abba

PREFACE

Globally, it is believed that music is food to the soul for the human race. Modern research has also proved that music can actually stimulate the productive capacities of animals (cattle, goats); birds (chicken, etc); insects (bees, etc) to produce higher yields once exposed to soft and orderly music. Music has been a motivating mechanism, and an instrument for healing and worship in shrines, palaces, but above all the worship of the God of gods.

The 15th and 16th Centuries in Europe have been known as the Renaissance (rebirth of human creativity). It was a period of exploration and adventure: consider the voyages of Christopher Columbus (1492); Vasco da Gama (1498); and Ferdinand Magellan (1519 – 1522). This was an age of curiosity and individualism too. This can be seen in the remarkable life of Leonardo da Vinci (1452-1519) who was a painter, sculptor, architect, engineer, scientist, and a fine musician as well. Renaissance was a period when an intellectual movement called Humanism was born. This focused on human life and accomplishment; but with no concern about the afterlife in heaven or hell.

On the contrary, the renaissance in music occurred between around 1400 – 1600. Just like with other arts, the horizon of music was greatly expanded with the invention of printing: widening the circulation of music, the number of composers and performers also increased. In keeping with the Renaissance ideal of the universal man, every educated person was expected to be trained in music. The church is became an important patron of music and musical activity gradually shifted to courts and palaces: kings, princes, and dukes competed for the finest composers. Around this time, musicians enjoyed a higher status and pay than ever before; composers were no longer contented to remain unknown; like any other artists, they sought credit for their work.

During the Renaissance, music was an important leisure activity; every educated person was expected to own and play a musical instrument but also be able to read musical notation. In the Renaissance as in the Middle Age, vocal music was more important than instrumental music because during renaissance humanistic interest in language influenced vocal music in a new way. As a result, an especially close relationship between words and music was established at that era. Renaissance composers wrote music to enhance the meaning and emotions of the text; "when the words express weeping, pain, heart break, sighs, let harmony be full of sadness" wrote Gioseffo Zarlino, a music theorist of the 16th Century. These composers often used words so as to paint musical representations of specific poetic images, for example words descending from heaven might be set to a descending melodic line and running might be heard with a series of rapid notes.

In conclusion, music has come a long way and therefore there is a need to preserve and also learn to read music in the eyes of the composers and their intended functions for this music; stories behind the song/ hymn composition. This publication is intended to highlight the background stories of selected golden hymns and gospel songs so as to enliven our congregational singing today. This will help us to learn to sing with a purpose and more insight, keeping in mind the circumstances that occasioned the composition of a certain song. I can't forget Martin Luther's quote (one of the founding fathers of the Protestantism, "God has His gospel preached also through the medium of music".

General Background to the Book

Christian hymns inspire us as we sing them in seasons of praise, prayer, and affirmation of major doctrines of the faith. Stories behind these hymns draw us into the lives of the writers and composers, and leave us with solemn admiration and profound respect for their talent and faithful endurance

The early English hymn writer, Isaac Watts, was greatly dissatisfied with the congregational singing in the churches of his day. In the preface to his Hymns of 1707, he wrote: "While we sing the Praises of our God in his Church, we are employed in that part of Worship which of all others is the nearest similar to Heaven; and 'tis pity that this of all others should be performed the worst upon Earth. . . . To see the dull Indifference, the negligent and the thoughtless Air that sits upon the Faces of a whole Assembly while the Psalm/ hymn is on their Lips, might tempt even a charitable Observer, to suspect the enthusiasm of inward Religion, and 'tis much to be feared that the Minds of most of the Worshippers are absent or unconcerned: . . . But of all our Religious earnestness, singing is the most delightful and divine Sensations that does not only flat our Devotion, but too often awakens our Regret, and touches all the Springs of Uneasiness within us."

Luther had strong convictions about the use and power of sacred music. He expressed his convictions in this way,

> "If any man despises music, as all fanatics do, for him I have no liking; for music is a gift and grace of God, not an invention of men. Thus it drives out the devil and makes people cheerful. Then one forgets all wraths, impurity and other device." Again, "The Devil, the originator of sorrow, anxieties and restless troubles, flees before the sound of music almost as much as the Word of God."

In another place, "I wish to compose sacred hymns so that the Word of God may dwell among the people also by means of songs." Finally, Luther wrote, "I would allow no man to preach or teach God's people without a proper knowledge of the use and power of sacred song."

Study Aids with a Practical Focus

This publication has been simplified for the reader so as to get the best out of its practical life and devotional resources for daily life. There are six classifications of the hymn and gospel songs background stories depend on their broad categories; and the book has been organised along those classifications for simplicity purposes, including:

i) Praise Songs:

These songs talk about God's miracles; His workings through our daily lives; our response to His goodness by shouting and dancing to praise Him. Simply put, responding to what God has done for us or seen us through. These are the following:

1. Amazing Grace
2. How sweet the name of Jesus sounds
3. Because He lives
4. Sweeter as the years go by
5. In my heart there rings a melody
6. Since Jesus came into my heart
7. Near to the heart of God
8. O happy day!
9. Tis so sweet to trust in Jesus
10. Rock of Ages
11. What a Friend we have in Jesus
12. My Jesus, I love Thee

ii) **Worship Songs:**

These songs express and manifest God's glory; creative power; His holiness. Simply put, singing about "who/what God is". These include:

1. O worship the King
2. O God our help in Ages past
3. I sing the Almighty power
4. Love Divine, all loves excelling
5. How great Thou art
6. Holy, Holy, Holy
7. The Messiah (The Hallelujah Chorus)

iii) **Discipleship Songs:**

These songs are about evangelism (the good news about Christ- life, resurrection, redemption, divine ministry in heaven, etc). They focus on Christianity; inviting/ mobilizing fallen humanity to Christ. These comprise of:

1. Jesus shall reign
2. There is power in the Blood
3. Tell me the story of Jesus
4. Take the name of Jesus
5. What a day that will be
6. Standing on the promises
7. I love to tell the story
8. Tell me the old, old story
9. We've heard (Jesus saves)
10. Stand up! Stand up for Jesus

11. The old rugged Cross
12. How firm a Foundation
13. A might Fortress
14. He lives
15. Beneath the Cross of Jesus
17. Chief of sinners
18. I gave my life for thee
19. Were you there when they crucified my Lord
20. More about Jesus

iv) Christian Living & Virtues Songs:

These songs are in the themes of: prayer, dedication, pleading, judgment, family life, etc. Most of them are played with a low tempo that implies thoughtfulness and a calm ambiance for spiritual needs. These are a function of:

1. Open my Eyes
2. Lord, I hear of showers of blessings
3. He leads me
4. Is my name written there?
5. T'is love that makes us happy!
6. God will take care of you
7. We know not the hour
8. Just as I am
9. Rescue the perishing
10. Come Thou fountain
11. Peace, be still
12. All the way my Saviour leads me
13. It is well with my Soul
14. I surrender all
15. I must tell Jesus
16. Lord, I a coming home

v) **Extraordinary Occasions Songs:**

These songs are used on special/ unique ceremonies for the church, these include: baptism, weddings, funerals, offerings, Holy Communion, and when dedicating either children or church ministers. Among others, these are:

1. I shall know Him
2. Nearer my God to Thee
3. Jesus, keep me near the Cross
4. Bringing in the sheaves (Sowing in the morning)

vi) **Benedictions & Doxologies Songs:**

These songs are aimed at: wishing/ bidding farewell to God's people with blessings; in a special way glorying God's protection, providence and faithfulness toward His people. These include:

1. God be with you till we meet again
2. Praise God from whom all blessings flow

vii) **Lay-Out of the Texts (Songs)**

Each song is organised in the following way:

- It begins with a simple biography of the author(s).
- It is followed by the circumstances that occasioned his/her composition of the song in question.
- Then, it is by a "devotional" in the form of Scriptures that either inspired his/her composition or that are in line with the song's spiritual resources (theology).
- Finally, the text is wound up with the life application lessons from the song that we need to draw from: the author's biography; the circumstances of the song's composition; and the Scriptural resources of the song.

Key to Abbreviations of Hymn Books:

CH   -   Church Hymnal

SDAH -   Seventh-Day Adventist Hymnal

CS   -   Christ in Song

A & M -   Oresmus Hymnal: Hymns Ancient & Modern 861 - 1874

NB: Luganda (local language) Titles refer to hymn titles in the SDA Church's Luganda hymnal called "Enyimba za Kristo"

In reference to my writing of this master-piece, I would happily love to use George Orwell's rationale for authorship. He said, "Putting aside the need to earn a living; there are four great motives for writing:

'Sheer egoism'- the desire to seem clever, to be talked about or even remembered after death, etc.

'Aesthetic enthusiasm'- the desire to share an experience which one feels is valuable and ought not to be missed. (Such as my musical experience that I feel worth sharing).

'Historical impulse' – the desire to find out true facts about something and store them up for posterity. (Hence, unearthing stories behind the glorious hymns about our Eternal God).

'Political purpose' – the desire to push the world in a certain direction. (By impressing on my readership the beauty & overwhelming experiences of hymn writers and other world personalities that can guide our spiritual & physical lives).

1. O WORSHIP THE KING
(Ka Tumusinze Mukama Waffe)
A & M 156   CH 75

This hymn was written by Sir Robert Grant, a Scottish Anglican who, because of his father's association with the East India Company, was born in India in 1779. Robert's father, Charles Grant supported Wilberforce, an early and effective opponent of slavery. Both father and son served as members of Parliament and directors of the East India Company. Grant (1778-1838) was born in India but moved back to England when he was seven years old. He became a lawyer at age 29, a Member of Parliament at 48 and was elected Judge Advocate General at 54. At age 56 he was knighted and then appointed Governor of Bombay, India, where he died at the age of 60. He was also a devout evangelical Christian who took every opportunity to share the Good News. He was a financial supporter of missionaries, and was loved by the people of India, who established a medical college in his honour. Several of Grant's writings, prose and poetry, were published during his lifetime. After his death, his brother gathered 12 of Grant's poems into a book titled Sacred Poems. One of those poems, O Worship the King, was set to music by Johann Michael Hadyn and has appeared in church hymnals ever since. Robert wrote this hymn in 1833, a year before being appointed Governor of Bombay, a position that he held until his death.

This hymn was inspired by a 16th century hymn by William Kethe; a hymn that was also inspired by Psalm 104. On reading Psalm 104 alongside the words of this hymn, there are several correspondences, such as:

i) The psalm (v.2) speaks of God as "wrapped in light as with a garment," and the hymn speaks of God "whose robe is the light."

ii) The psalm (v.2) says, "You stretch out the heavens like a tent," and the hymn uses the phrase, "whose canopy space."

iii) The psalm (v.3) says, "You make the clouds your chariot, you ride on the wings of the wind." The hymn says, "His chariots of wrath the deep thunderclouds form, and dark is his path on the wings of the storm."

The first two verses of the hymn celebrate God's glory while the last two verses celebrate God's love and providence. God's greatness and God's loving providence — go together. God's power makes it possible for him to provide for us "frail children of dust" (v.4.).

This gentleman was so busy a man of the world to concern himself with hymns, as one would suppose. He was a Parliamentarian for many years; and like his father, he was deeply concerned with social issues of the community in which he lived. Robert accepted a high position in the East India Company; and later he was asked to be governor of Bombay, which he accepted from 1834. As governor, he had opportunity to put his social concerns into practice, for the poverty and spiritual condition of the common people were appalling.

Through his persistent efforts a bill was eventually passed which emancipated England's Jews. He fought for other minority groups, too. In the meantime, he was a strong supporter of world missions and influential among evangelicals in the Church of England. He sketched a history of the East India Company but still he found time to write hymns.

This is considered one of the greatest hymns of worship in the English language that have not only survived but have withstood the test of time. In poetic form it describes God's impact upon the lives of His children over the years. The Ancient of Days is our Shield and Defender from all the attacks of Satan. He is our Maker who cares for us with His bountiful care. He is our Redeemer whose mercies are tender. And this great King is also our Friend. And we, who are the frail children of dust, feeble and frail, can put our faith in Him for He will not fail. And with this knowledge and experience we should daily sing gratefully of His power and His love. I pray that as we contemplate and sing the words of this profound hymn that the Lord may fills us with awe, praise and thanksgiving as we worship the King. But also, we ought to learn to concern/ identify ourselves with the societal issues such as poor health, alarming poverty, injustices, promiscuity, ungodly living, and lawlessness just as Robert Grant did during his meaningful short stay in this world. This is because that is the real contribution and impact we live in our community for the relatively short time we spend with them in this mortal life.

> *O worship the King, all glorious above,*
> *O gratefully sing His power and His love;*
> *Our Shield and Defender, the Ancient of Days,*
> *Pavilioned in splendor, and girded with praise.*
>
> *O tell of His might, O sing of His grace,*
> *Whose robe is the light, whose canopy space,*
> *His chariots of wrath the deep thunderclouds form,*
> *And dark is His path on the wings of the storm.*
>
> *Thy bountiful care, what tongue can recite?*
> *It breathes in the air, it shines in the light;*
> *It streams from the hills, it descends to the plain,*
> *And sweetly distills in the dew and the rain.*
>
> *Frail children of dust, and feeble as frail,*
> *In Thee do we trust, nor find Thee to fail;*
> *Thy mercies how tender, how firm to the end,*
> *Our Maker, Defender, Redeemer, and Friend*

2. O GOD, OUR HELP IN AGES PAST
(Mukama Gwe Kifo Kyaffe)
A & M 197   CH 81

Isaac Watts was the son of a schoolmaster, and was born in Southampton, July 17, 1674. He is said to have shown remarkable precocity in childhood, beginning the study of Latin, in his fourth year, and writing respectable verses at the age of seven. At the age of sixteen, he went to London to study in the Academy of the Rev. Thomas Rowe, an Independent minister. In 1698, he became assistant minister of the Independent Church, Berry St., London. In 1702, he became pastor. In 1712, he accepted an invitation to visit Sir Thomas Abney, at his residence of Abney Park, and at Sir Thomas' pressing request, made it his home for the remainder of his life. It was a residence most favorable for his health, and for the prosecution of his literary labors. He did not retire from ministerial duties, but preached as often as his delicate health would permit.

Isaac Watts (1674-1748) captured the infinite timelessness of God in contrast to the momentary nature of humanity in his metrical paraphrase of Psalm 90, "O God, our help in ages past"—a classic hymn for the Christian community world over. Watts is often called the "Father of English hymnody"—that is, hymns on a wider range of topics rather than musical versions of the psalms in the English language. Before him, congregational songs focused almost exclusively on singing strict metrical versions of the psalms. Following the Scripture closely was of the utmost importance and was religiously upheld. Metrical psalms, a product of the Reformed tradition, generally could neither add to nor delete anything from the psalm as found in the Bible. The result was that some rather awkward phrasings were tolerated in order to meet the strict demands of poetic meter.

The direct opposite between God and humanity is the primary message of Psalm 90 and Watts' paraphrase of a psalm of Moses, which originally consisted of nine stanzas, and the hymn is highly ranking as one of the finest Watts' more than 600 hymns in his musical composition career. Returning to J.R. Watson, he correctly observes, "This is one of Watts's greatest hymns on the human condition, setting the shortness of life and the littleness of human beings against the timeless greatness of God.... who has been our help [in the past] and hope [in the future]."

The first verse gives us every assurance we need: God is our help, our hope, and our home. This does not casually dismiss our fears and troubles. They are, and always will be, very real. But it does assure us that even if we cannot feel the immediate comfort, or even when all we can do is lament, we have a God that withstands the storms of the life and the tests of time, and who protects us and hears our cries. Isaiah 41:9-10 says, "I took you from the ends of the earth, from its farthest corners I called you. I said, 'You are my servant'; I have chosen you and have not rejected you. So do not fear, for I am with you; do not be dismayed, for I am your God. I will strengthen you and help you; I will uphold you with my righteous right hand."

In the contemporary world, this could furthermore be emphasized by the fact that we are living in an age when more and more of our Christian beliefs are being challenged by a growing liberal society. Law makers and especially judges continue to hack away at many Biblical principles which believers have always held to, leaving many of us in despair of what will happen next. Many years ago Christianity also faced a dark and uncertain future in England when Queen Anne forced through Parliament the Schism Act designed to severely limit religious freedom. And this situation, it is believed contributed to Isaac Watts writing this favorite hymn, "Our God Our Help In Ages Past." I envisage that the words brought comfort and new courage to the Christians who were facing a fearful and uncertain future just like we do currently in the 21st Century. And my prayer is that the hymn would do the same for us, generations later as we deeply meditate upon the words of this great hymn that is filled with spiritual metaphors: He is our shelter in the stormy blast; His arm is sufficient for all our needs and His defense is sure; and while things are constantly changing around us, He was before the hills were formed and He will be the same for endless years. And He is our help and hope and our guard until the day that He takes us to our eternal home. What a tremendous truth and a powerful reminder to all of us in the uncertain days characterized by terrorism, social injustices, religious indifference and selfishness that we face. May the good God, our help impress us with the power of this truth as we pilgrim in this deadly world so that we can keep on looking up to our eternal shelter as did the Hebrews during their exodus from the Egyptian bondage.

(1) *Our God, our help in ages past,*
Our hope for years to come,
Our shelter from the stormy blast,
And our eternal home.

(2) *Under the shadow of Thy throne*
Still may we dwell secure;
Sufficient is Thine arm alone,
And our defense is sure.

(3) *Before the hills in order stood,*
Or earth received her frame,
From everlasting Thou art God,
To endless years the same.

(4) *A thousand ages in Thy sight*
Are like an evening gone;
Short as the watch that ends the night
Before the rising sun.

(5) *Time, like an ever rolling stream,*
Bears all its sons away;
They fly, forgotten, as a dream
Dies at the opening day.

(6) *Our God, our help in ages past,*
Our hope for years to come,
Be Thou our guard while life shall last, And our eternal home.

3. JESUS SHALL REIGN WHERE'VER THE SUN
A & M 196   (Yesu Alifuga Wonna)

Isaac Watts was a prolific hymn writer who is credited with writing over 600 hymns during his lifetime. Many of them are still used today to worship and praise the same Savior Watts loved and served. Born on July 27, 1674 at Southampton, England, he was the eldest of nine children. His father was a Dissenter from the Anglican Church and on at least one occasion was thrown in jail for not following the Church of England. Isaac followed his father's strongly biblical faith. He was a very intelligent child who loved books and learned to read early. He began learning Latin at age four and went on to learn Greek, Hebrew, and French as well.

On the contrary, it is said that Watts was not attractive to look at since he was frail and often sickly. His head seemed too large for his short five foot body. His small, piercing eyes and hooked nose did not enhance his appearance. A lady once fell in love with Isaac by reading his poetry and a correspondence between them followed. When she met him face to face, however, she was very disappointed, even though he fell in love with her. He asked her to marry him, but her reply was, "Mr. Watts, I only wish I could admire the casket (jewellery box) as much as I admire the jewel." Watts never married, though the two remained good friends for over 30 years.

This hymn was written in 1719 and is said to be his paraphrase of Psalm 72. "Jesus Shall Reign Where're the Sun" is considered by many to be the first great missionary hymn. It was written at a time when the church was doing little missionary work. Watts envisioned a day when Jesus would reign throughout the world - wherever the sun shines - from shore to shore. His original verses envisioned a time when all people - princes, savage tribes, people of all languages, even infants - would praise Jesus' name. Current hymnals have modernized the language somewhat and generally reduced the original 14 verses to five. Since the days of Watts, the Gospel has spread throughout the world and believers can be found almost everywhere, despite the fact that many must worship in secret for fear of persecution or even death. But there still are tribes and people groups who need to be reached with the good news. May we be active in spreading this message to all, whether it be by actually going ourselves or by supporting, with our money and prayers, those who are going. May we do our part to help see "the prisoner leap to lose his chains and the weary find eternal rest", as we have hopefully experienced ourselves. And there will be a time when people from every nation gather to worship, praise and bring honour to our King.

When this stirring hymn was written in 1719, the evangelical missionary movement that we know in our time had scarcely begun. And in 1779 William Carey became one of the first to try to persuade Christians to carry the gospel message to heathen countries of the world. The writer of this missionary hymn, Isaac Watts, was certainly quite prophetic when he paraphrased this text from Psalm 72. It is still considered one of the finest missionary hymns ever written and has been sung in countless native tongues.

This hymn is linked to the Pauline writings in Romans 1:16-17, "For I am not ashamed of the gospel of Christ: for it is the power of God unto salvation to everyone that believes; to the Jews first and to the Greek. For therein is the righteousness of God revealed from faith to faith: as it is written, the just shall live by faith."

This is evidenced by a story that is told about a certain South Sea Island tribe that had been so hostile to missionaries that whenever they would dare to go there for evangelism, they would feast on them (cannibalism) since it was a deadly community. This prompted the missionary society administration to write them off, judge them and prohibit any missionary activities in that region. However, one retired missionary received an inspiration from God sending him for missionary/ evangelistic activities in that same community. On approaching and sharing his inspiration with the missionary society administrators, they thought he was crazy and in need of mental rehabilitation since it was common knowledge that the region was a deadly zone. They used also avenues to dissuade him from that initiative but seemed determined not until he was made to sign a will and a document to show that he was responsible for his fatal decision, and that for them they have no liability on his life. Him, along with a team of choirs embarked on their navigation on the Indian Ocean but just few meters to the shore he stopped the vessel, and ordered the choirs to sing the hymn "Jesus shall reign wherever". This incited their chief/ king to come out of their usual hideouts in the forest along the sea shores to apologize for their past misconduct and pleaded with the singers to take his word and accept to disembark so as to come teach them how: to sing such glorious songs; to live by faith and have hope; but also to learn to love and appreciate modern civilization. Later on, in the South Sea Islands in 1862, 5,000 primitive people sang this hymn as the king abolished their native laws and established a Christian constitution.

(1) Jesus shall reign where'er the sun
Does his successive journeys run;
His kingdom stretch from shore to shore,
Till moons shall wax and wane no more.

(2) To Him shall endless
prayer be made,
And praises throng to crown His head;
His Name like sweet perfume shall rise
With every morning sacrifice.

(3) People and realms
of every tongue
Dwell on His love with sweetest song;
And infant voices shall proclaim
Their early blessings on His Name.

(4) Blessings abound
wherever He reigns;
The prisoner leaps to lose his chains;
The weary find eternal rest,
And all the sons of want are blessed.

(5) Let every creature rise and bring
Peculiar honors to our King;
Angels descend with songs again,
And earth repeat the loud amen!

4. THERE IS POWER IN THE BLOOD

The text was written and the tune was composed both by Lewis Edgar Jones (1865-1936). Graduating from Moody Bible Institute in the same class with well-known revival evangelist Billy Sunday, Jones became active in YMCA work which he did for the rest of his life. Hymn writing was his hobby, and in his spare time he produced quite a few songs that were published. His most famous song, "There Is Power in the Blood," was produced while Jones was attending a camp meeting at Mountain Lake Park, MD, in 1889.

The blood of Jesus is one of the most vital and fundamental themes of Christianity that often seems to be missing in modern churches today since most have gotten carried away by the prevalent secularism, materialistic and self-seeking tendencies that are practically consuming the world and any remaining Christian values and standards. This is evident in services of most Christian churches that are filled with prayers, offerings and thanksgiving for, among others: getting visas, juicy jobs, pregnancies, social approval and marital happiness. All of which are not bad per se but what is unbecoming is the fact that they are now taking the rightful position of "The power in the blood of our Lord Jesus Christ". The blood is vital and necessary because the Scripture tells us that without the shedding of blood there is no remission of sins. It was Jesus who came to this earth and shed His blood at Calvary, making our salvation possible. He willingly was the perfect Lamb, the sacrifice for our sins, and without that sacrifice we would be eternally lost. But unfortunately it is often and progressively becoming a ridiculous and in fact despicable practice to share a message that emphasizes blood not only in social gatherings but even some Christian churches due to the looming secularism and religious syncretism in the 21st Century.

The modern church "worshipper" gets turned off by that and so many sermons and music avoid that topic. And yet, without the blood, the church has no relevant message to share to a lost world. It is the power in the blood that frees us from the burden of sin and gives us victory and power for living. There is wonder working power in the precious blood of the Lamb, Christ Jesus which this hymn clearly articulates. I trust that you have been redeemed by the power of the blood of the Lamb, lest we forget the importance of it and the sacrifice that was involved, and may we ever be thankful that Christ did this for us.

(1) Would you be free from the burden of sin?
There's pow'r in the blood, pow'r in the blood;
Would you o'er evil a victory win?
There's wonderful pow'r in the blood.

Chorus
There is pow'r, pow'r, wonder-working pow'r
In the blood of the Lamb;
There is pow'r, pow'r, wonder-working pow'r
In the precious blood of the Lamb.

(2) Would you be free from
your passion and pride?
There's pow'r in the blood, pow'r in the blood;
Come for a cleansing to Calvary's tide;
There's wonderful pow'r in the blood.

(3) Would you be whiter, much
whiter than snow?
There's pow'r in the blood, pow'r in the blood;
Sin-stains are lost in its life-giving flow;
There's wonderful pow'r in the blood.

(4) Would you do service for Jesus your King?
There's pow'r in the blood, pow'r in the blood;
Would you live daily His praises to sing?
There's wonderful pow'r in the blood.

5. TELL ME THE STORY OF JESUS
(Nyonyola Ebya Yesu)
CH 534

Fanny Crosby penned the words and music was added by John R. Sweney in 1880. There really isn't a particular event that seems to have motivated the blind hymn writer to write these words. It is known that she learned to play multiple musical instruments, write poetry, speak publicly, and organize missionary works in poverty-stricken urban areas in the U.S. We know that even among all the positives in her life, there were also many disappointments, including, in 1880, when Crosby had apparently separated from her husband, Alexander Van Alstyne. That year she chose to live in a slum in Manhattan, apparently choosing this path as part of a recommitment to better serve the poor in domestic missionary work. Living in a slum, helping the poor, she focused attention not on herself and what she could do, but instead on Him, whose story she dearly loves to tell. The words of this hymn sound like someone sharing the Gospel with the needy, despised and afflicted, who were without hope. It is believed that some of these poor folks were among the first to hear and appreciate her poem put to music. What's a group that's struggling to survive day-to-day looking for? Someone who shares their pain, who also overcame, someone they could understand.

I'm tempted to conceive the idea that such an ambiance of the low-life was in part the motivation to the writing of this hymn hence the vocabulary of: afflicted, despised, fasting, anguish and pain; as they are likened with Christ's earthly experience. But we, too, need to have this story written on our hearts, and a new vision of who Jesus is so that as we review this story, we may ask the Lord to stir us, to renew us and to create a passion for sharing His story and His love to others.

Sometimes when things are often repeated to us they begin to lose their impact as they pass to be a monotonous and boring tale. I vividly take this opportunity to remember my late grandparents who used to tell us the same old stories in their experiences not realizing that they had already on numerous accounts told us the same old "monotonous tales", and while we could continue to politely listen to them, our minds would wander and the details become less interesting to us.

In the same vein, for those of us who have grown up in a Christian environment, we could be equally tempted do the same thing with the Old old story of Jesus (Gospel) that has so far lasted for millennia. The rhetoric questions that would be asked could be as follows: Does it still excite us and stir us like it did when we first heard it? Does the Gospel message grip us as it used to? As a matter of fact, as Christians, we should never tire of the stories of Jesus. We should long to hear them over and over and be continually thrilled by who He was, what He did and His love for each of us.

(1)   Tell me the story of Jesus,
Write on my heart every word.
Tell me the story most precious,
Sweetest that ever was heard.
Tell how the angels in chorus,
Sang as they welcomed His birth.
"Glory to God in the highest!
Peace and good tidings to earth."

Chorus
Tell me the story of Jesus,
Write on my heart every word.
Tell me the story most precious,
Sweetest that ever was heard.

(2)   Fasting alone in the desert,
Tell of the days that are past.
How for our sins He was tempted,
Yet was triumphant at last.
Tell of the years of His labor,
Tell of the sorrow He bore.
He was despised and afflicted,

(3)   Tell of the cross where they nailed Him,
Writhing in anguish and pain.
Tell of the grave where they laid Him,
Tell how He liveth again.
Love in that story so tender,
Clearer than ever I see.
Stay, let me weep while you whisper,
Love paid the ransom for me.

6. TAKE THE NAME OF JESUS WITH YOU
(Twalanga Erinnya Lya Yesu)
CH 523

Many a great hymns were written by persons who lived with serious physical challenges and among the most notable ones: Fanny J Crosby, Arabella K Hanky, Annie J Flint, among others. And so is the case for Lydia Baxter, born in Petersburg, New York, she was saved as a young person (1809 - 1874) was a bedridden invalid for much of her life, but that didn't keep her from leading a life full of service and encouragement. It is said that she and her sister were once responsible for establishing a Baptist Church in Petersburg, New York. After her marriage, she and her husband moved to New York City where her home became known as a gathering place for preachers, evangelists, and Christian workers who would come to her for inspiration and advice. It is said that a visit to her sickroom was not so much to comfort her as to receive encouragement for their own lives and spirits. Whenever she was questioned about her cheery disposition, despite her physical limitations, she would reply, "I have a very special armor. I have the name of Jesus. When the tempter tries to make despondent, I mention the name of Jesus, and he can't get through to me anymore." Throughout her lifetime she was known as an avid student of the Bible who loved to discuss the significance of scriptural names with her friends. She would inform them that Samuel means 'asked of God', Hannah--'grace', Sarah--'princess', and Naomi--'pleasantness'. But the name that meant everything to Lydia Baxter was the name 'Jesus'.

This golden hymn was written by Baxter on her sickbed, four years before her death in 1874 at the age of 65 years. William H. Doane composed the music for this text shortly after Mrs. Baxter wrote it, and the hymn was first published in the hymnal, Pure Gold, edited by Doane and Robert Lowry, in 1871. This hymn was widely used during the Moody-Sankey evangelistic campaigns, in the latter quarter of the nineteenth century. Although she wrote a number of other gospel hymns, this is the only one that remains in common use today. It has often been used in church services as a closing hymn since it provides an important reminder to go forth each day, taking His name with us, while sharing with others what He has done in our lives.

In one sense the hymn is really the personal testimony of Lydia Baxter's experiences with the name of Jesus throughout her life. His name is indeed precious and sweet and the only real hope of earth and joy of heaven. This reminds me of a scenario in the bible when the disciples asked Jesus what had caused the blindness of a certain unidentified man in the bible, as in their minds they had popular belief that misfortunes were as a results of God's retribution for the sinfulness of either the person in question or his parents for that case. But Christ calmly responded by giving them crucial Christian and real life lessons that at times such happenings occur so that God's providence, faithfulness and care can be revealed to the world through His divine workings. And Paul once responded in relation to his persistent sight problems that emanated from his encounter with Jesus on the way to Damascus, that Christ's grace is sufficient in that when Paul is either in good health or in death or whichever life situation, it is because of Jesus' goodness(2 Cor. 12:9, 10).

Lydia Baxter's life experience is only reminding us of such concrete Christian lessons that whatever the life situation, we ought to use it to bless others rather than to lament as those who don't have faith and hope, because Jesus uses such happenings to fortify not only our faith but also that of others we live with.

Rejoice in the Lord always, and again I say rejoice (Philippians

4:1ff), please read that chapter that Paul wrote while in the Roman dungeon as he was really nearing his death but didn't hesitate to exhort his brethren in Philipp, who were actually in their comfort, to rejoice in the Lord always and make known their needs to Him whose name they ought to walk with them.

Baxter's testimony, coupled with Paul's solacing message in Philippians 4:1-; remind me of a beautiful and rather inspiring text a friend of mine sent me one day about Arthur Ashe (a legendary Wimbledon Tennis Player:

Ashe was dying of the contemporary scourge of AIDS which he got due to infected blood that he received during a Heart surgery in 1983. Thus, he began receiving letters from his fans, one of which conveyed, "Why did God have to select you for such a bad disease?" To which Ashe replied:

50 Million Children started playing Tennis; 5 Million learnt to play Tennis; 500,000 learnt Professional Tennis; 50,000 came to Circuit; 5,000 reached Grand-slam; 50 reached Wimbledon; 4 reached the Semi-finals; and when I was holding the Trophy in my hand, I never asked God, "why me?". So, now that I'm in pain how can I ask God, "why me?"

The text continues......

Happiness keeps you sweet! Trials keep you strong! Sorrows keep you Human! Failure keeps you Humble! Success keeps you Glowing!

But only Faith keeps you Going!!

Sometimes you are unsatisfied with your life, while many people in this world are dreaming of living your life...

A child on a farm sees a plane fly overhead and dreams of flying. But a pilot on the plane sees the farm house and dreams of returning home. That's life so you ought to enjoy yours....

If wealth is the secret to happiness, then the rich should be dancing on the streets. But only poor kids (street kids) do that.

If power ensures security, then VIPs should walk unguarded. But those who live simple sleep soundly.

If beauty and fame bring ideal relationships, then celebrities should have the best marriages.

Live simple, walk humbly and love genuinely!!

(1) Take the name of Jesus with you,
Child of sorrow and of woe;
It will joy and comfort give you,
Take it then where'er you go.

Chorus
Precious name! Oh, how sweet!
Hope of earth and joy of heav'n;
Precious name! Oh, how sweet!
Hope of earth and joy of heaven.

(2) Take the name of Jesus ever,
As a shield from every snare.
If temptations round you gather,
Breathe that holy name in prayer.

(3) Oh, the precious name of Jesus,
How it thrills our souls with joy;
When His loving arms receive us,
And His songs our tongues employ.

(4) At the name of Jesus bowing,
Falling prostrate at His feet,
King of kings in heaven
we'll crown Him,
When our journey is complete.

7. AMAZING GRACE
SDAH 108

This popular hymn is the personal testimony of its author, John Newton, a slave trader before coming to Christ. For a better understanding of the author and the circumstances that led to the birth of the spiritual edifying song, kindly refer to the background of his other precious hymn "How sweet the name of Jesus sounds".

But it was God's amazing grace (God's Riches at Christ's Expense) that drew him from a life of sin to become a child of the King. Many of us now may not clearly appreciate how filthy slave trade was to our ancestors who encountered it then. I hardly watch movies and if I'm to do so, I'm rather picky in movies I do watch, such as: adventure films, comedies and detective kind of films. One day, I was somehow fortunate/ unfortunate to watch a Steven Spielberg Film titled AMISTAD which showcased events of 1839 summer, where 53 African slaves were being transported by a Spanish slave ship La Amistad to be traded in Europe. This movie would give you glimpses of how awful, dreadful and despicable slavery was that John Newton, although his career as a gospel minister regrets having had an experience in such a dehumanizing and degrading activity in his profile which would always make him feel unworthy to serve the great God of Justice. In fact, this hymn was used by Christians in that movie who were fighting against slavery in that era. Slaves were butchered, drowned, raped and dehumanized anyhow and at the discretion of the white slave traders with impunity and as if there was no God who would really intervene in such dreadful acts of sinful and selfish humanity.

It was while John was at Olney that he wrote over 280 hymns, including 'Amazing grace' and 'How sweet the name of Jesus sounds'. The first verse of 'Amazing grace' fittingly sums up John's spiritual history:

Hymn Stories For Our Contemporary Lifestyles

> *Amazing grace! How sweet the sound*
> *That saved a wretch like me!*
> *I once was lost, but now am found,*
> *Was blind, but now I see.*

> Let's learn not to quickly write off people spiritually due to their current behavior: foul-mouth; blasphemy; animosity; drunkenness; adultery; spiritual infidelity; corruption & theft etc. This is because Christ Jesus didn't write John off but was so tolerant with him leading him to repentance & into a church minister but also a great hymn writer that we up to the 21st Century admire. It is a common practice to quickly judge our brethren, despise them & finally write them off as if we, personally have had untainted & faultless life profiles

Today this hymn is sung at so many public events, especially funerals and memorial services. The Pauline writings to the church in Rome; Romans 3:23-25 remind us that, "For all have sinned and have fallen short of God's glory; being justified freely by His grace through the redemption that is in Christ Jesus". How I pray that our hearts would be open to the truth and power of this grace.

(1) Amazing grace! How sweet the sound
That saved a wretch like me!
I once was lost, but now am found;
Was blind, but now I see.

(2) 'Twas grace that taught
my heart to fear,
And grace my fears relieved;
How precious did that grace appear
The hour I first believed!

(3) Through many dangers,
toils and snares,
I have already come;
'Tis grace hath brought me safe thus far,
And grace will lead me home.

(4) The Lord has promised good to me,
His Word my hope secures;
He will my Shield and Portion be,
As long as life endures.

(5) Yea, when this flesh
and heart shall fail,
And mortal life shall cease,
I shall possess, within the veil,
A life of joy and peace.

(6) The earth shall soon
dissolve like snow,
The sun forbear to shine;
But God, who called me here below,
Will be forever mine.

(7) When we've been there
ten thousand years,
Bright shining as the sun,
We've no less days to sing God's praise
Than when we'd first begun.

8. HOW SWEET THE NAME OF JESUS SOUNDS:
(Erinnya Lya Yesu Ddungi)
A & M 185   CH 150

This hymn was written by John Newton who is probably better known for his hymn "Amazing grace." John was born in 1725 and died in 1807. His father was a sea captain; his godly mother died when John was only 7 years old and all Christian influence was gone. He was press-ganged into the Royal Navy when he was 19 years old. He became a foul-mouthed, loose living sailor and was known on board ship for his constant blasphemy. When he was 23 years old, his ship, 'The Greyhound', ran into a violent storm, so much so that it seemed the ship would sink. In desperation, John cried out to God to save him. Amazingly to John, God did just that! The storm abated and the ship just managed to limp into Ireland. After repairs, it finally arrived in Liverpool. That experience marked the beginning of John's conversion.

By now, John was heavily involved in the slave trade and captained several slaving trips, though he began to be increasingly troubled about his role as a Christian in the slave trade. When he was 30 years old, and by now married, he left the sea and obtained his first land job as Tide Surveyor in Liverpool.

On his 33rd birthday, John told his wife he would spend the day in prayer and fasting for direction as to his future. He felt that would be as a minister in the Church of England. It wasn't until 6 years later that he was finally ordained in St. George's Church, Liverpool after having preached a 2 hour sermon for which duration, very few congregations in the modern day would stand that long sermon.

Shortly afterwards, John moved to be vicar of Olney in

Northampton shire. He died in 1807. It can only take an Amazing grace to transform Newton, once an infidel and libertine, a servant of slaves in Africa, and, by the rich mercy of our Lord and Savior Jesus Christ, to be preserved, restored, pardoned and appointed to preach the faith he had long labored to destroy.

It was while John was at Olney that he wrote over 280 hymns, including 'Amazing grace' and 'How sweet the name of Jesus sounds'.

'How sweet the name of Jesus sounds' is a demonstration of the amazing grace of God that a man, to whom for many years the name of Jesus was used simply as an oath, could pen such words. My dear readers, if you have never yet appreciated the sweetness of the name of Jesus, kindly learn through the words John Newton penned about it. The grace of God in Christ can save you as certainly as it did John Newton. Then you will be able to agree with Apostle Peter about the Lord Jesus, "Therefore, to you who believe, He is precious" (1 Peter 2:7).

Taking a clinical analysis of the first two verses of our hymn & let us review five different statements regarding the name of Jesus:

> *How sweet the name of Jesus sounds*
> *In a believer's ear!*
> *It soothes his sorrows, heals his wounds,*
> *And drives away his fear.*
>
> *It makes the wounded spirit whole,*
> *It calms the troubled breast;*
> *'Tis manna to the hungry soul,*
>
> *And to the weary rest.*
> *Dear name, the rock on which I build,*
> *My shield and hiding place,*

My never failing treasury,
Filled with boundless stores of grace.

Jesus! My Shepherd, Guardian, Friend,
My Prophet, Priest and King
My Lord, my life, my way, my end!
Accept the praise I bring

Weak is the effort of my heart,
And cold my warmest thought,
But when I see Thee as Thou art,
I'll praise Thee as I ought.

It soothes his sorrows

The Lord Jesus perfectly understood and entered into the deep sorrow of Martha and Mary. To demonstrate that He was indeed the Son of God, come in resurrection power, Jesus calls Lazarus out from the dead and restores him to his sisters. Then in chapter 12, we see Martha, Mary and Lazarus happily making a feast for Jesus. And so we, today, in our sorrows can go and tell Jesus and find that He can indeed soothe our sorrows.

Heals his wounds

We live today in a world of wounded and broken lives – not just the material wounds of high speed living, of war and destruction – but the spiritual wounds of broken homes, of drug addiction, of hopelessness. In Jesus' day, society may have looked very different from ours, at least on the surface, but the wounds were still there, and He dealt with them.

When, at the beginning of His public ministry, Jesus stood up in the synagogue at Nazareth to read, He read from the book of the prophet Isaiah: "The Spirit of the LORD is upon Me, because He has anointed Me to preach the gospel to the poor. He has sent Me to heal the broken hearted, to preach deliverance to the captives and recovery of sight to the blind, to set at liberty those who are oppressed, to preach the acceptable year of the Lord" (Luke 4:18-19). Some 600 years earlier, Isaiah, by the Spirit of God, had been moved to pen those words of the coming Messiah, words that were so completely fulfilled in the Lord Jesus. How many wounded and broken hearts then, and since then, have found healing in Him!

And drives away his fear

Years later, His disciple John, who had gone through that storm with Him, wrote, "There is no fear in love; but perfect love casts out fear" (1 John 4:18). Today, the Lord Jesus invites us to share that same loving confidence in His Father and, in this way, He drives away our fear.

The Lord Jesus has not given us a trouble free and fear free world in which to live. All of us, at some time or other, will encounter the storms of life. But as He whispers to our souls His own words, "Peace, be still!", then we can indeed find that He will drive away our fears.

'Tis manna to the hungry soul

The line, of course, can only be understood by reference to the provision God made for the Israelites when He brought them out of Egypt, through the wilderness, to the Promised Land. In the wilderness, God miraculously provided them with manna, ('bread from heaven' as God describes it to Moses) and with quails. Without this provision, the Israelites would have all perished (Exodus 16.)

As Christians, we too are on a journey - through this world on our way to heaven. This world has no spiritual food to offer that will sustain us on this journey. Only the Lord Jesus can do that! In John 6:33, the Lord Jesus says, "The bread of God is He who comes down from heaven and gives life to the world". He goes on to show that not only is He the One to whom we must come to receive God's gift of eternal life, but He is the One who alone can sustain that life.

And to the weary rest

The invitation of the Lord Jesus still holds good today: "Come to Me, all you who labor and are heavy laden, and I will give you rest. Take My yoke upon you and learn from Me, for I am gentle and lowly in heart, and you will find rest for your souls. For My yoke is easy and My burden is light" (Matthew 11:28-30). The Lord Jesus is the only one who can give rest of conscience if we come to Him confessing our sins and receiving Him as our Savior. But He also gives rest of heart as we go through this troubled world in the assurance of His constant care over us. Peter urges us, "Casting all your care upon Him, for He cares for you"
(1 Peter 5:7).

A story is told that one of Newton's last messages from the pulpit in 1805 ended with his shout that "Jesus Christ is precious", and that the assembled worshippers sang this hymn at his request. I presume its words must have conveyed something Newton thought was important for people to hear in his 80th year. He evidently hadn't forgotten his transgressions, judging from his poem's words, but Newton knew how to find his way out of moral prison. And, maybe he saw in the faces of his hearers some of the guilt they still carried with them, and that they needed this name; as an escape as well.

9. OPEN MY EYES
SDAH 326

Clara H. Scott (1841-1897) provided us with a hymn of consecration that shares this need and prayer. Over the years she wrote many hymns and in 1882 she published the Royal Anthem Book, the first volume of choir anthems ever published by a woman. Three collections were issued before her untimely death, when a runaway horse caused a pushchair accident in Dubuque, Iowa. The text of "Open My Eyes" was written in 1895 shortly before Scott's death.

Each stanza reveals an increasing receptiveness to the "Spirit divine." Open eyes lead to "glimpses of truth." Open ears lead to "voices of truth." An open mouth leads to sharing the "warm truth everywhere." An open heart leads to sharing "love to Thy children." Scott has given us not only a list of organs through which we may receive and project truth and love, but also provides the method in her refrain. Maybe in these days of busy schedules and noise and distractions all around us, we need to make this our daily prayer ... open our eyes, open our ears and then open our mouths. Maybe we need to take time to silently wait for Him to do this. The hymn might be old, but the need has never been greater than now in an era where people watch things which are spiritually destructive, people listen to fables and concocted stories with no truth in them, and people create stories, all sorts of blasphemy, insults that they speak without remorse. Why not make this your life prayer and find some time just to be silent before the Lord and listen to what He has to share with you.

Clara's hymn connects so well with Paul's second epistle to the Corinthians 5:7, "For we walk by faith, not sight."

In 2001, I was diagnosed with rather critical eye defects in the form of allergies and the opticians advised that I should use eyeglasses if not I would risk turning blind or something close to that. This really threatened not only my life then but also my perspective towards the future because I did not anticipate how much trouble I would actually have during that time since I couldn't read and write and work on my computer as I do so regularly. And while I wasn't blind by any means, the experience made me appreciate so much more what blind folks deal with daily. And at times I just wanted to cry out, "Lord open my eyes so that I could see". But as difficult as physical blindness may be, spiritual blindness is really bad news. And while we might not be spiritually blind, at times our vision can become dim and lose it sharpness. A more serious prayer is to ask the Lord daily to open our eyes so that we may see the Truth that He has for us.

This reminds me of a story about a young lady called Hellen Keller who was deaf, blind and mute; totally handicapped but regardless of all these misfortunes, she studied and became a professor. She was so popular, so intelligent that masters and PhD students would always consult with her when working on their theses and dissertations. One day, journalists approached her and asked her a crucial question that, we also, ought to ask ourselves today, "Tell us mum Keller, what you think is the greatest tragedy one can ever face?? She replied, "The greatest tragedy is to have eyes without vision." They asked again for the difference between sight and vision; (so reflective before answering) she said, "Sight is the ability to see things as they are but vision is the ability to see things as they could be." So many people have physical eyes but they are just good-for-nothing eyes because they can't help them to figure out what things could be (opportunities, blessings and strengths in what apparently appear to be commonplace to many folks) so as to fully exploit them for their betterment and that of the kingdom of God.

*(1) Open my eyes, that I may see
Glimpses of truth Thou hast for me;
Place in my hands the wonderful key
That shall unclasp and set me free.*

*Chorus
Silently now I wait for Thee,
Ready my God, Thy will to see,
Open my eyes, illumine me,
Spirit divine!*

*(2) Open my ears, that I may hear
Voices of truth Thou sendest clear;
And while the wave notes
fall on my ear,
Everything false will disappear.*

*(3) Open my mouth, and let me bear,
Gladly the warm truth everywhere;
Open my heart and let me prepare
Love with Thy children thus to share.*

10. BECAUSE HE LIVES
SDAH 526

Not many hymns date back less than half a century just like this hymn in question but due to its deep and rich spiritual resources, I'm convinced to share it with you. In effect, I would love to inform you, in case you didn't know, that Bill and Gloria Gaither have had a major impact upon Gospel music during the past century. Our lives have been touched in many ways by their ministry and music. But they have experienced some rough times throughout their lives just like any mortal being in this sinful world.

During the late 1960s, while expecting their third child, they went through a rather difficult time. While Bill was recovering from mononucleosis, he and Gloria and other members in their church family were the objects of false accusations and belittlement. It was a time of torment, especially for Gloria. With all the challenges facing her family, the thought of bringing another child into the world was taking its toll on her. She recalls sitting in their living room in agony and fear on New Year's Eve. Across the nation the "God is dead" movement was increasing and drug abuse and racial tension were growing. This time was characterized as the "Existentialism era" where it was widely believed that God was dead due to high prevalence of: wars, aggravated homicides, epidemics; this led to indifference and decline in moral & ethical values in the world. It was around this time that people strongly believed their existence is only and basically because they had no option since all circumstances tried to see them dead for reasons not even known to these people they have failed to die due to high prevalence of positive population checks according to Malthusian theory of population (deliberate reduction of population through various mechanism), and contraceptives that were used for abortion arising from an era code-named "the Baby boom". This was the aftermath of the two world wars that had claimed/ destroyed a multitude of human life to the point that world leaders offered incentives for their people to produce more children and boost population growth for a variety of economic and non-economic objectives.

But suddenly, and unexpectedly, she was filled with a sweet, calming peace. Like an attentive mother bending over her baby, it was as if her heavenly Father saw her and came to her rescue. Her panic gave way to calmness and assurance and the realization that the future would be just fine, left in God's hands. The power of Christ's resurrection was reaffirmed. To Gloria, it was "life conquering death" as joy once again permeated the fearful circumstances of their lives. And this was how the Southern Gospel song, "Because He Lives" came to be written. The first verse reminds us of Christ's death, burial, and resurrection. In the second verse we see the life of a new baby and sense the assurance that Christ alone can give. The third verse reminds us of the final victory when we are taken to glory. So as we realize that God holds the future and makes life worth living for all who trust in Him, we can face tomorrow with all the uncertainty it brings.

Memory text: Judges 13:12, "And Manoah said 'when your words come true, what kind of rules should govern the boy's life work?"

Ellen G. White in her publication "Child Guidance" exhorts that, "as marriage unites two hearts and lives in love, and a new home is created, an early concern of its founders is that the children which grace this new home shall be properly nurtured". She adds that, Manoah's question of old," How shall we order the child?" is thoughtfully pondered by parents today as they look into the face of the precious and helpless gift entrusted to their care.

Besides, this hymn story reminds me of one story that is believed to be among the saddest stories ever told in Hollywood. It is about **Sylvestar Stallone**, one of the biggest and most famous American movie superstars in history. He was a struggling actor by all definitions; one time, he got so broke that he stole his wife's jewellery and sold it for survival. Life became so complicated that he ended up homeless, to the point of sleeping at the New York bus station for 3 days since he couldn't pay rent or food. He lowest point came when he opted to sell his long time friend (his dog) at a drinking bar to any stranger since he had no money to feed it anymore, and he sold it USD 25 only. He narrates that he walked away crying but two weeks later, he saw a boxing match between Mohammed Ali and Chuck Wepner and that match gave him the inspiration to write the script for the famous movie, ROCKY. He wrote the script for 20 hours, and tried to sell it and got an offer for USD 125,000 for the script but he had one request, **he wanted to STAR** in the movie as the main Actor **Rocky himself.** But the studio said NO because they wanted a Real Star, and added that, "he looked funny and talked funny", so he left with his script. A few weeks later, the studio offered him USD 250,000 for the script but he declined the offer. They even offered USD 350,000 and he still refused since they wanted the movie but not him. He said NO, since he had to be in that movie. After a while, the studio agreed to give him USD 35,000 for the script and let him star in it! The rest became history, since the movie won the Best Film Editing at the prestigious Oscar Awards, and he was nominated for Best Actor, and the movie ROCKY was even inducted into the American National Film Registry as one of the greatest movies ever! Incidentally, the first thing he bought was his dog at USD 15,000 because he loved his dog so much that he stood at the drinking bar/ store for 3 days waiting for the man who had bought it. This was done after a lengthy explanation and pleading for the repurchase of his dog. And today, the same Stallone who slept in streets and sold his dog just because he couldn't feed it anymore is one of the greatest movie Stars in world history. You know, being broke is really bad basically if you had a big and wonderful dream but don't have what it takes to implement it. In such a state, opportunities will pass by, just because you are insignificant; people will want your products but not you; doors will be shut on you; people will steal your glory and crash your hopes. You will do odd jobs for survivals; unable to feed yourself; and you may end up sleeping in the streets; and this happens so often in our lives regardless.

On the contrary, never let others crush your dreams; you ought to keep on dreaming even when they turn away or shut all doors on you. No one knows what you are capable of doing except yourself; people will judge you by how you look and what you have but please fight on for your place in history, for your glory. This might mean, just like Stallone, selling your clothes and sleeping with the dogs. All that is ok, as long as you are still alive, and trust me, your story is not yet over. Apostle John emphasizes that, "For whatever is born of God overcomes the world. And this is the victory that has overcome the world—our faith" 1 John 5:4

(1) God sent His son, they called Him Jesus
He came to love, heal, and forgive.
He lived and died to buy my pardon,
An empty grave is there to prove my Savior lives.

Chorus
Because He lives, I can face tomorrow.
Because He lives, All fear is gone.
Because I know He holds the future,
And life is worth the living just because He lives.

(2) How sweet to hold a newborn baby,
And feel the pride and joy he gives.
But greater still the calm assurance,
This child can face uncertain days because He lives.

(3) And then one day I'll cross the river,
I'll fight life's final war with pain.
And then as death gives way to victory,
I'll see the lights of glory and I'll know He lives.

11. I SING THE ALMIGHTY POWER OF GOD
(Obuyinza Bwo Bungi Nnyo)
CH 93

Isaac Watts was the author of this hymn, along with many other favorites such as "Joy to the World," "O God, Our Help in Ages Past," and "When I Survey the Wondrous Cross."

As a young man, Watts served as pastor of the Mark Lane Church in London. However, in 1712, at the age of 38, he suffered an emotional breakdown that limited his activities. However, he was blessed to have good friends to take care of him, in particular Sir Thomas and Lady Abney, with whom he lived for the last 36 years of his life.

Even though he never married, Watts enjoyed children and published the first hymnal designed expressly for children. This hymn, "I Sing the Mighty Power of God," was one of the hymns that he wrote for that hymnal and he intended it to be sung by children.

While the words of this hymn sound nothing like the songs being written for children today, it speaks of God making mountains rise; spreading the flowing seas abroad; building the haughty skies. It tells of a sun that rules the day; a moon that shines at God's command; and stars that all obey. These are word images that children can, at some level, understand since the biggest part of children learning should always be in form of music and images which help them to conceptualize concrete and abstract realities in their early life. Watts knew that, by singing words such as these over and over again, children would come to understand something of God's creation, his providence, and his love which consequently who serve to ignite a solid relationship between children and their creator/ savior.

More than a century down the road, Christ inspired his own (Ellen G. White) to pen these concrete parenting lessons to a world that no longer perceived children as a valuable asset but a liability or a distraction, "God wants every child of a tender age to be His child, to be adopted into His family......... As soon as a child can love and trust his mother, then he can love and trust Jesus as the Friend of his mother, loved and honored" (Child Guidance, ...)

What Watts could not have understood, is that his hymns would also be sung gladly by adults and in places of which he had never known, and for centuries after his death (Watts died in 1748).

The early English hymn writer, Isaac Watts, was greatly dissatisfied with the congregational singing in the churches of his day. In the preface to his Hymns of 1707, he wrote:

"While we sing the Praises of our God in his Church, we are employed in that part of Worship which of all others is the nearest similar to Heaven; and 'tis pity that this of all others should be performed the worst upon Earth. . . . To see the dull Indifference, the negligent and the thoughtless Air that sits upon the Faces of a whole Assembly while the Psalm/ hymn is on their Lips, might tempt even a charitable Observer, to suspect the enthusiasm of inward Religion, and 'tis much to be feared that the Minds of most of the Worshippers are absent or unconcerned: . . . But of all our Religious earnestness, singing is the most delightful and divine Sensations that does not only flat our Devotion, but too often awakens our Regret, and touches all the Springs of Uneasiness within us" (Louis, 1915).

Fortunately, Watts was not content merely to state what was lacking in the congregational singing of his day. He began writing hymns and eventually produced more than 600. Contemporary hymnals still include a significant number of Watts' hymns.

This hymn is rich in theology with an attractive and easy to sing folk melody. It was inspired by Watts' thorough knowledge of

God's creative power (the basics for our living) in Genesis 1:1ff "In the beginning God created the heavens and the earth............"

This song serves to impress such valuable knowledge and realities to the young generation that has grown up in an era of total confusion in almost everything but basically about who actually created the universe. This is due to the significant effect that Darwin's theory of evolution, coupled with the atheistic views of refuting the fact that Christ Himself created the universe out of nothing but His love for humanity. It is quite strange that at almost the same time that God was inspiring His own modern generation prophetess Ellen G. White to write in emphasis and clarification to His creative power of the whole universe, Charles Darwin (a onetime believer in Christianity) was writing to undo/ refute God's creative power. Incidentally, research has shown that a lot more followers (hundreds of millions) have believed Darwin's theories world-over (not even two centuries old) since they are even integrated in education systems contrary to Christianity/ Godliness that has lasted for a lot more centuries but with just a few millions of believers.

This further remind of a popular story about a certain household which had a very inquisitive boy (just like any kid from a good background). One day, this boy felt unsatisfied with a longing of knowing how humanity came into existence; he approached the dad and asked him how both the dad and the boy happened to come to the world. In response, the dad (a strong believer in God's creative power) narrated the whole creation story as revealed in Genesis 1 & 2, showing how through love God created humanity including them too. The boy went away somewhat convinced but not so long, a belief that maybe the father left out something begun perturbing him; this saw him head to the mum so as to get her take on the same question.

Surprisingly, the mother gave him another creation account (as engineered by Charles Darwin) that humanity came from primates/apes and that thanks to modernity and technology, man has evolved to the current appealing looks without a tail and animal features. Very disillusioned, the boy rushed back to the father so as to accuse him of not being truthful in his creation account; but the father (also disappointed by the wife's commentary) told the boy that, "maybe your mother's ancestors/lineage comes from apes/monkeys but my lineage comes from Adam and other ancestors who were created by a Loving Lord for a divine purpose; and that is where you also come from."

> *I sing the mighty power of God*
> *That made the mountains rise,*
> *That spread the flowing seas abroad,*
> *And built the lofty skies.*
> *I sing the wisdom that ordained*
> *The sun to rule the day;*
> *The moon shines full at His command,*
> *And all the stars obey.*
>
> *I sing the goodness of the Lord*
> *That filled the earth with food;*
> *He formed the creatures with His Word,*
> *And then pronounced them good.*
> *Lord, how thy wonders are displayed,*
> *Where'er I turn my eye,*
> *If I survey the ground I tread,*
> *Or gaze upon the sky.*
>
> *There's not a plant or flower below,*
> *But makes Thy glories known;*
> *And clouds arise, and tempests blow,*
> *By order from Thy throne;*
> *While all that borrows life from thee*
> *Is ever in Thy care,*
> *And everywhere that we can be,*
> *Thou, God, art present there.*

12. LORD, I HEAR OF SHOWERS OF BLESSINGS (EVEN ME)
(Emikisa Gyo Mukama)
CH 208

Words: Elizabeth Codner, 1860

Music: William B. Bradbury, 1862

As regards this hymn, Codner gave a personal testimony of how the hymn came into existence,

"A party of young friends, over whom I was watching with anxious hope, attended a meeting in which details were given of the beginning of revival in Ireland. They came back greatly impressed. My fear was lest they should be satisfied to let their own fleece remain dry, and I pressed upon them the privilege and responsibility of getting a share in the outpoured blessing. On the Sunday following, not being well enough to go out, I had a time of quiet communion. These children were still on my heart, and I longed to press upon them an earnest individual appeal. Without effort words seemed given to me, and they took the form of the hymn which I then wrote-

"Lord I hear of showers of blessing."

I had no thought of sending it beyond the limits of my own circle, but, passing it on to one and another, it became a word of power, and I then published it as a leaflet "

"Even me" is one of those hymns that has become disconnected in popular use; at least for many who sing it from its original doctrinal context. The fervent plea for the Lord's individual attention, heard especially in the middle stanza's "Pass me not" (which is clearly echoed in Fanny Crosby's 1868 hymn of that name), reflects the Wesleyan belief in seeking for a dramatic conversion experience. Codner's own statement places the origin of her text in the midst of news of the great Methodist revival in Ireland, and tells us that she was driven by her desire for the "young people" on her heart to find a similar experience.

"Even me" can be read in this more generic sense as well. The essential thought of "pass me not"--a seeming fear that the Lord will overlook us--can be compared to the poetic exaggeration used by David: "How long, O LORD? Will You forget me forever? How long will You hide Your face from me?" (Psalm 13:1). It is evident that David knew that God cannot forget, and we know that God will not overlook any of His children; but in the realization of our desperate need for Him, we might speak in such pleading terms.

The phrase "showers of blessing" comes from Ezekiel 34:26b: "And I will send down the showers in their season; they shall be showers of blessing." The prophecy in this chapter encouraged the Jewish exiles to look forward to a great restoration, when they would be led by "one shepherd, My servant David" (v. 23). To an agricultural society in a land with such low and infrequent rainfall, and yet simultaneously subject to flash flooding when rain did come, there was a special sweetness to the idea of a period of good soaking showers. It was a time of new growth, and of nourishment of the existing plants.

This context makes real meaning in the contemporary world that is at the height of effects from global warming that has fundamentally disorganized climatic seasons in the Sub-Saharan Africa where I live exposing us only to desperation and great uncertainty. My country (Uganda) is an agro-based economy where production is basically dependent on showers of rainfall for a better livelihood. Unfortunately, global warming has adversely affected seasonal sequences that we, farmers, really crave for a time when showers of rainfall would soak the ground so that we can have hope for the future through agricultural yields. Whenever signs of such showers manifest on the sky, I admit that I have cheered aloud for a promising-looking thundercloud, hoping for something to break the scorching sunshine that has practically been destroying any existing vegetation.

In the physical world we deal with droughts by tapping reservoirs, and to some extent God has put reservoirs of mercy among us. There are fellow Christians whose experiences of God's mercy overflow into the lives of others and refresh them. There are also the beauties God has placed around us in nature, and in those things in life that are true, honourable, just, pure, and lovely (Philippians 4:8). But these are not the source of mercy itself, and just as the physical reservoirs of water must be replenished from the rains, we need that mercy that comes from God himself. He is the "Father of Mercies" (2 Corinthians 1:3), both the originator of mercy and the One who excels all others in this quality. There is mercy enough for every sinner, if they will seek it according to God's will. And for the Christian, there is mercy always at hand for the asking: "Let us therefore come boldly unto the throne of grace that we may obtain mercy, and find grace to help in time of need" (Hebrews 4:16).

Stanza 1:
Lord I hear of showers of blessing
Thou art scattering full and free,
Showers the thirsty land refreshing:
Let Thy mercy fall on me.
Even me, even me,
Let Thy mercy fall on me.

Stanza 2:
Pass me not, O gracious Savior,
Let me live and cling to Thee;
I am longing for Thy favor:
Whilst Thou'rt calling, O call me.
Even me, even me,
Whilst Thou'rt calling, O call me.

Stanza 3:
Love of God, so pure and changeless,
Blood of Christ, so rich, so free,
Grace of God, so strong and boundless,
Magnify them all in me.
Even me, even me,
Magnify them all in me.

13. WHAT A DAY THAT WILL BE

It was written by **Jim Hill**. His mother-in-law became very sick; and he was a very new Christian at the time. One day when he was coming home from work, he was asking God why this was happening to his mother-in-law. Then he said, words just started filling his mind, but he did not have anything to write the words down. So when he got home he got out of the car, looked down and there was an old piece of cardboard. So he picked it up and wrote down the words to "What A Day That Will Be." The first person that Jim Hill sung the song for, was his sick mother-in-law. Since then the song has been an anthem of encouragement many times for many people.

This hymn can be enhanced by John's apocalyptic writings in Revelation 21:4, "And God shall wipe away all tears from their eyes; and there shall be no more death, neither sorrow, nor crying, neither shall there be any more pain: for the former things are passed away."

Last Camp meeting (September 2014) as we were enjoying the spiritual and life skills packages that are organized on an annual basis, we were introduced to the awful news that our best friend (late Elder Ssebandeke Moses) had suddenly and unexpectedly died while ministering during the camp meeting at SDA Church Kajjansi due to electrocution. I still have such a difficult time believing this happening and we will miss him. In addition to my beloved sister Jemimah who passed in 2005 who I truly adored, my dear grandparents, uncles, aunts and friends but what gives me joy is the hope that they all died in Christ. What a day that will be when we see Jesus and our dear relatives and friends once again. What a thrill it is to have that assurance as we face the loss of their friendship and companionship here on earth. Whenever I sing and contemplate over this song, I simply can't help but strongly anticipate that glorious day when there will not be any heartache, disappointments and craving for our loved ones that have departed from us in this mortal life. I feel overjoyed when I think of that blessed day when I, with my own eyes, shall see and look upon the face of the One who saved me by His grace. Brethren, how will that day look like when He takes me by the hand and leads me through the Promised Land?? What a day, glorious day that will be!!

(1) There is coming a day
When no heartache shall come
No more clouds in the sky
No more tears to dim the eye
All is peace forever more
On that happy golden shore
What a day, glorious day that will be.

Chorus
What a day that will be
When my Jesus I shall see
And I look upon His face
The One who saved my by His grace
When He takes me by the hand
And leads me through the Promised Land
What a day, glorious day that will be

(2) There'll be no sorrow there
No more burdens to bear
No more sickness, no pain
No more parting over there
And forever I will be
With the One who died for me
What a day, glorious day that will be.

14. SWEETER AS THE YEARS GO BY

The lyrics and music were written by Leila N. Morris (1862-1929), who became blind in her early fifties, but that didn't keep her from writing. It is said that she had a 28-feet long blackboard with large music staff lines. Using this special board she was able to see enough to help her write hymns. In all, she wrote more than 1,000 hymn texts as well as many of her tunes. Her handicap didn't keep her from doing this and being productive for God. As it is popularly said "disability is not inability"; actually these days it is no longer referred to as *disability* but in a gentle vocabulary it is called being *physically-challenged*. Even with her blindness, Mrs. Morris found that her Lord did become sweeter to her as the years went by. Richer, fuller, deeper, Jesus' love is sweeter, sweeter as the years go by. May this also be your experience regardless of what you are going through now (be it that you are physically, emotionally, spiritually, intellectually and socially challenged)!!!

In 2013, one of my grandmothers passed away at the age of 105 years with still a very sound mind. Incidentally, she could recall people she had seen 5 years earlier and much as she had been bedridden for close to 7 years and her sight was really fading way but her intellect was still good enough so that she could make rational analyses and also differentiate a variety of voices. During her burial, multitudes (even including some relatives) were filled with awe on hearing that she had lasted for a whole 105 years of her fruitful life. Can you guess why people were rather shocked that she lived that long?? Yes, it is because time does fly, in other words, sweeter the years go by that at times we might not take the care to realize it. To highlight this reality in life, let me give you these life experiences: this year (2015), my parents will make 33 years in marriage; I'll make 32 years of age; my wife and I made 5 years in marriage; and many more things happen in our lives without really noticing how time goes by and yet it really runs so fast. But here comes the rhetoric question, "Where did the years go?" And in all these relationships and life stages (my parents marriage; my marriage; my life), they are better and closer today than ever before. And that is the testimony shared by this hymn, "Sweeter As The Years Go By".

No matter how long you have served the Lord *or you have been in church/ faith*, I hope that this is also your testimony. During Paul's time and ministry, he along with other apostles were anticipating Christ's return which prompted him once to remark that Jesus' return would find him alive but he died centuries ago and Christ has not returned as yet. On the contrary, it does not matter how long and fast the time goes by but how fruitful and valuable your long/ short life has been to yourself, the church, the community and above all to our glorious Lord who promised a great reward for a life well lived. This life ought to appreciate the "wonderful love that sought us when we were lost in sin; the wondrous grace that brought us back to His fold again; the heights and depths of mercy, far deeper than the sea; and higher than the heavens, our theme shall ever be."

(1) Of Jesus' love that sought me, when I was lost in sin;
Of wondrous grace that brought me back to His fold again;
Of heights and depths of mercy, far deeper than the sea,
And higher than the heavens, my theme shall ever be.
Sweeter as the years go by, sweeter as the years go by,
Richer, fuller, deeper, Jesus' love is sweeter,
Sweeter as the years go by.

(2) He trod in old Judea life's pathway long ago;
The people thronged about Him, His saving grace to know;
He healed the broken hearted, and caused the blind to see;

*And still His great heart yearneth in love for even me.
Sweeter as the years go by, sweeter as the years go by,
Richer, fuller, deeper, Jesus' love is sweeter,
Sweeter as the years go by.*

*(3) 'Twas wondrous love which led Him for us to suffer loss,
To bear without a murmur the anguish of the cross;
With saints redeemed in glory, let us our voices raise,
Till Heav'n and earth reecho with our Redeemer's praise.
Sweeter as the years go by, sweeter as the years go by,
Richer, fuller, deeper, Jesus' love is sweeter,
Sweeter as the years go by.*

15. IN MY HEART THERE RINGS A MELODY

The text and tune were written by Elton M. Roth (1891-1951). Roth was a well known musician in his day that wrote and published many anthems and over 100 hymns. It was while assisting with evangelistic meetings in Texas on a hot summer day in 1923 that the words and music for this hymn suddenly came to him. He says that this new song that God gives us may have no words whatever, no melody, no rhythm, and no harmony. This is a "song in the heart". The hymn title is based on the words of the apostle Paul in Ephesians 5:19, "...........singing and making melody in your heart to the Lord". And the song is basically describing a "melody of love". Mr. Roth recalled, "That evening I introduced the song by having more than 200 boys and girls sing it at the open air meeting, after which the audience joined in the singing. I was thrilled as it seemed my whole being was transformed into song." And ever since then, thousands of believers have joined in joyfully singing about the melody that rings in your heart because of what Christ has done for each of us. Despite your circumstances today, I hope this melody is ringing within your heart.

This hymn is further connected to Psalms 40:1-3, "I waited patiently for the Lord; and he inclined unto me, and heard my cry. He brought me up also out of an horrible pit, out of the miry clay, and set my foot upon a rock, and established my goings. And he has put a new song in my mouth, even praise unto our God: many shall see it, and fear, and shall trust in the Lord."

As I reflect upon church music as I was growing up, there were some hymns that I loved to sing not only because of their message but due to their rhythms, and some hymns I would associate them to issues in life that made me happy. What a joy to know that Christ can put a melody of love in your heart and that the words can ring there despite what is happening around you. And as is so common in these older hymns, the last verse talks about heaven where the courts of glory will ring with glorious harmony. I love that thought and look forward to that day.

It is quite unfortunate that in this era, many a children and youths have hearts that are filled with melodies not of love and glory of God but of poisonous content such as beef (hatred), promiscuity, obscenity, rivalry, among other social toxins in form of "music" that has filled all households, schools, social gatherings and even some churches. This has promoted lawlessness, moral degradation and loss of Christian values in our society which are filled with people bearing Christian names incidentally. Research has shown that music has a direct contribution to one's personality and character but the critical question that is of profound interest to consumers, parents, spiritual leaders and even political leaders is; which type of music does one consume?

(1) I have a song that Jesus gave me,
It was sent from heaven above;
There never was a sweeter melody,
'Tis a melody of love.

Chorus
In my heart there rings a melody,
There rings a melody with heaven's harmony;
In my heart there rings a melody;
There rings a melody of love!

(2) I love the Christ who died on Calv'ry,
For He washed my sins away;
He put within my heart a melody,
And I know it's there to stay.

(3) 'Twill be my endless theme in glory,
With the angels I will sing;
'Twill be a song with glorious harmony,
When the courts of heaven ring.

16. STANDING ON THE PROMISES
SDAH 518

Russell Kelso Carter (1849-1928) was a star athlete of a military academy and an excellent student academically, who went on to be a successful teacher and coach. He then spent several years as an ordained Methodist minister, after which he went to medical school. He spent the last of his professional years as a doctor of medicine. Carter was also a musician and songwriter. In 1886, he co-edited a hymnbook which included Carter's most famous hymn, Standing on the Promises which was written while he was serving as a professor (of chemistry and mathematics) at the Pennsylvania Military Academy. There is a profound lesson that I have learnt from Carter's life (that may be worthwhile a lesson in the modern competitive world), and that is endeavouring to train oneself to be as multi-skilled as humanly possible. Whenever I have gotten the opportunity to train communities in career development, I have always emphasized this reality in life since no one knows what really will help him/ her to survive in this so dynamic and competitive world. I have been sharing with them that God has blessed me with a couple of skills, just like Russell Carter, such as: being a sportsman (playing basketball, table tennis, volleyball, badminton and football); being a multilingual (speaking English, French, Spanish, Luganda, Swahili, Kinyarwanda, etc); being an entrepreneur and educator; being a musician; being an orator and a writer/ author; being a leader, a husband and dad; and last, professionally being a financial economist/ investment professional. These skills coupled together can and by God's grace would help one and one's household to live/ survive in this so dynamic world.

The music, composed by Carter as well, has the kind of bright marching style that must have been familiar at the academy. Although Carter was a professed Christian most of his life, it wasn't until a crisis with his natural heart that he began to understand the reality and power of Bible promises. At age 30, his health was in critical condition and the physicians could do no more for him. Carter turned to God for help and healing. He knelt and made a promise that healing or no healing, his life was finally and forever, fully consecrated to the service of the Lord. It was from that moment that the written Word of God became alive to Carter. Over the course of the next several months his strength returned, and his heart was completely healed. Carter lived another healthy 49 years.

The hymn is related to an encouragement from Isaiah 40:31, "But those who wait on the Lord shall renew their strength; they shall mount up with wings like eagles, they shall run and not be weary, they shall walk and not faint."

Life's storms may threaten to sweep us away at times, but when we choose to stand upon the promises of God, we have found a place of safety, a place where the footing is forever firm. With confidence we say, "the Word of our God stands forever" (Isa. 40:8). It is rather disheartening to note that despite our God's unwavering faithfulness and consistence in keeping His promises, we, as human, have categorically chosen the contrary that is never to keep our word / promises such as King Hezekiah did during his extended reign as King of Israel (Isaiah 39:1ff). And this is widely evident in the broken promises of living a faithful Christian life according to our calling; broken marriage vows due to infidelity against our spouses; unfaithfulness in returning tithes and offerings which would indicate our gratitude to God's providence; failure to fulfil political and leadership promises; promising all of things to our children yet fulfilling a lot of nothing;

and besides, possibly the worst of all the failure to live to the basic expectations of our communities. On the contrary, to believe the word of God and obey it is to anchor our lives to the invincible rock of God's truth and to live a life of not only faithfulness to our promises but also filled with God's peace that surpasses all human understanding. What a great place to stand as we strive this year in a world that is filled with despair and uncertainty.

(1) Standing on the promises
of Christ my King,
through eternal ages let his praises ring;
glory in the highest, I will shout and sing,
standing on the promises of God.

(2) Standing on the promises that cannot fail,
when the howling storms of doubt and fear assail,
by the living Word of God I shall prevail,
standing on the promises of God.

(3) Standing on the promises of Christ the Lord,
bound to him eternally by love's strong cord,
overcoming daily with the Spirit's sword,
standing on the promises of God.

Chorus
Standing, standing,
standing on the promises
of Christ my Savior;
standing, standing,
I'm standing on the promises of God.

4() Standing on the
promises I cannot fall,
listening every moment
to the Spirit's call,
resting in my Savior as my all in all,
standing on the promises of God.

17. SINCE JESUS CAME INTO MY HEART

The text was written by Rufus Henry McDaniel who was born in 1850 and started preaching at age nineteen. He then became a minister with the Christian Church (Disciples of Christ) in 1873. In 1914, following the untimely death of his son, Rufus penned these words as an expression of his faith and hope. The tune (McDaniel) was composed by Charles Hutchinson Gabriel who had it copyrighted. Despite the fact that the song is exactly one hundred years old since its first publication in 1915, its message is still relevant for today. If Jesus indeed has "come into our heart", there should be obvious changes. This song talks about some of these changes and as we sing it we should be reminded of these. And our hearts should be thankful to a great God who through the sacrifice of His Son has made all of this possible. And as is often the case in these older songs, there is a final verse which talks about heaven and that City where we shall one day dwell. And that indeed should fill us with hope, joy, and expectation as we "onward go". So, if you've experienced these changes, then join us in singing this song throughout this week.

Among the Pauline writings to the Corinthians, is a great lesson and inspiration to this hymn. "Therefore, if anyone is in Christ, he is a new creation, old things have passed away; behold all things have become new" 2 Corinthian 5:17. But also Proverbs 29:25, "The fear of man brings a snare, but whoever trusts in the Lord shall be safe."

What made the Hebrews (Israelites) different from other nations was not so much as their way of thinking, or even their "spiritual" and abstract theological views. It was concrete choices in life about, among other things: food they ate; the rest (Sabbath); the natural environment; and their relationships with neighbours and family that made them "holy" or "set apart" from all other nations; choices which were basically centred on the law and its principles. That is why when we live a responsible life of obeying God's law; we manifest a wonderful change in our life since Jesus will have come into our hearts so that we can live by faith in Him.

This song reminds us further that when Jesus comes into our hearts we become new creatures, old things have become new. And this brings to my mind that story that I didn't complete about a certain community in the Indian Ocean's South Sea Island which was initially a heathen society that used even to feast on human flesh of those who could visit them but later adopted Christian constitution due to allowing Jesus to come into their territory. One unique story has it that, one day a certain old man was on his veranda busy studying his bible when a proud young man can and begun making fun of him and wondering why on God's earth one would waste his valuable time reading a useless book like what the old man had. Then, the Mzee (old man) calmly stood up and got hold of the young man's hand, and led him into one of the rooms in his house which had an old cupboard filled with souvenirs of their past life including lots of human bones of every type and "genre" of those they had feasted on. The reckless young man was so frightened but he could not escape so he begun pleading with the old man to forgive him, yet the old man courteously told him, "it is only that book you are despising that wrought a wonderful change in my life (our lives), and had it not been that change (of Christ coming into my heart), you would definitely be finished today!" This rhymes so we with McDaniels' inspiration of the song in question "What a wonderful change in my life has been wrought since Jesus came into my heart; I have light in my soul for which long I have sought, since Jesus came into my heart."

*(1) What a wonderful change in my life has been wrought
Since Jesus came into my heart;
I have light in my soul for which long I have sought,
Since Jesus came into my heart.*

Chorus
*Since Jesus came into my heart,
Since Jesus came into my heart;
Floods of joy o'er my soul like the sea billows roll,
Since Jesus came into my heart.*

*(2) I have ceased from my wand'ring and going astray,
Since Jesus came into my heart;
And my sins which were many are all washed away,
Since Jesus came into my heart.*

*(3) I'm possessed of a hope that is steadfast and sure,
Since Jesus came into my heart; And no dark
clouds of doubt now my pathway obscure,
Since Jesus came into my heart.*

*(4) There's a light in the valley of death now for me,
Since Jesus came into my heart;
And the gates of the City beyond I can see,
Since Jesus came into my heart.*

*(5) I shall go there to dwell in that City I know,
Since Jesus came into my heart;
And I'm happy, so happy as onward I go,
Since Jesus came into my heart.*

18. I LOVE TO TELL THE STORY
(Nsanyuka Okwogera)
CH 518

Katherine Hankey was born in 1834, the daughter of a wealthy English banker. Early in life Katherine caught the evangelical concern from her father and she began organizing Sunday school classes for rich and poor throughout London. All of the royalties received from these publications were always directed to a foreign mission project. She never married and spent her entire life in religious activities; teaching bible classes for working women. In 1866, she experienced a serious illness. During a long period of recovery she wrote a lengthy poem on the life of Christ.

The poem consisted of two main sections, each containing fifty verses. The first section of the poem was entitled "The Story Wanted." and it was from this part of her poem that she later adapted the words for another of her familiar hymn texts, "Tell Me the Old, Old Story." Later that same year, while still recovering from her illness, she completed the second part of her poem on the life of Christ. This continuation to the first section was entitled "The Story Told." From these verses came the text for "I Love to Tell the Story," Being musically inclined, Kate also composed her own tunes for these two texts. Her hymns received little notice, however, when used with this music. The following year, 1867, a large international YMCA convention was held in Montreal, Canada. One of the speakers at the convention, Major General Russell from England, closed his emotionally charged message to the delegates by quoting the verses from Miss Hankey's two hymn texts. In the audience that day was a noted American gospel musician, William H. Doane, composer of more than 2,000 gospel songs. Mr. Doane was greatly moved by these lines and promptly composed musical settings for both texts. Later a new musical setting, which replaced Doane's music for "I Love to Tell the Story," was composed by William G. Fisher, a Philadelphia musician and piano dealer. Fischer also added the refrain for the hymn, "I Love to tell the story! 'Twill be my theme in glory-to tell the old, old story of Jesus and His love."

This hymn is linked to the Pauline writings in Romans 1:16-17, "For I am not ashamed of the gospel of Christ: for it is the power of God unto salvation to everyone that believes; to the Jews first and to the Greek. For therein is the righteousness of God revealed from faith to faith: as it is written, the just shall live by faith."

Hankey's song explains four crucial reasons as to why she so loves to tell the story of Jesus:

1. "Because I know it is true". Unlike many fables, concoctions, myths and lies that are prevalent in this fallen world with very little to be taken as absolutely true even from the closest and dearest ones, she strongly believes that the story of Christ is really grounded in truth. Thus, making it worth sharing with whoever can listen since all authoritative world history books testify of this reality.

2. "Because it satisfies my longing as nothing else can do." Fame, riches, highly-specialized education can be good for daily mortal living but research has shown that they have caused more longing and desperation in hearts of those who trust in them and that is why committing suicide, homicides, depression are so characteristic of the western civilized countries which would appear to be a paradox. The reality is that it is only the story of the goodness of our Lord Jesus Christ that can quench or satisfy our longing, and that is why Hankey is so proud to tell the story.

3. "Because some have never heard the message of salvation from God's own holy word". Most congregations have resorted to telling their audiences other stories such as: healing chronicle illnesses, getting visas, earning marriages, amassing wealth, and bearing children; which are not bad in themselves but

giving them more importance than the beloved story of Jesus' message of salvation is really losing the point.

4. "Because those who know it, best seem hungering and thirsting to hear it like the rest." How truly I wish we could have such a hunger for the story of Jesus but not for: stories about the despicable and reckless stories about "celebrities"; political gossip and ideologies; sports contests and betting; among other not so beneficial stories.

The story that Hankey so dearly loves to tell is not confined to only 33 years of Jesus' earthly life but: begins in glory of God's eternal presence; to the description of the actual work of our creation; to initiatives and actions to save His people. This storyline climaxes when God's Eternal Son renounces His glory to live as a human to minister to our needs, and show us how we should live and serve Him.

(1) I love to tell the story of unseen things above,
Of Jesus and His glory, of Jesus and His love;
I love to tell the story, because I know 'tis true,
It satisfies my longings as nothing else would do.

Chorus
I love to tell the story,
'Twill be my theme in glory,
To tell the old, old story
Of Jesus and His love.

(2) I love to tell the story, more wonderful it seems
Than all the golden fancies of all our golden dreams;
I love to tell the story, it did so much for me,
And that is just the reason I tell it now to thee.

(3) I love to tell the story, 'tis pleasant to repeat,
What seems each time I tell it more wonderfully sweet;
I love to tell the story, for some have never heard
The message of salvation from God's own holy Word.

(4) I love to tell the story, for those who know it best
Seem hungering and thirsting to hear it like the rest;
And when in scenes of glory I sing the new, new song,
'Twill be the old, old story that I have loved so long.

19. TELL ME THE OLD OLD STORY
SDAH 196

We've already shared the story behind the writing of "I Love To Tell The Story" If you recall, Katherine Hankey wrote a lengthy poem on the life of Christ while she was recovering from a serious illness. It contained two main sections each containing fifty verses. The first part of the two sections was entitled "The Story Wanted". And the second part was, "Tell Me the Old, Old Story". I hope that we never get tired of hearing and sharing this story, the greatest story ever. The old, old story of Jesus and His love. The story that Christ Jesus makes us whole.

This hymn reminds me of a well compiled and comprehensive text which clinically analyses the death of Christ's Apostles; and the zeal, forbearance and faith they displayed during their persecution that would serve as both testimony and challenge to our contemporary Christianity:

> i) *Matthew: he suffered martyrdom in Ethiopia (on our African soils & neighbourhood) by being killed with a deadly sword.*
>
> ii) *Mark: he died in Alexandria, Egypt (still African soils & a country with whom we share the River Nile) after being dragged by the horses through the streets until his death.*
>
> iii) *Luke: he was hanged in Greece (a country whose economy is currently collapsing & in disarray, with threats of being expelled from the Euro-zone) as a result of his preaching to the lost.*
>
> iv) *John: he faced martyrdom when he was boiled*

in a huge container of cooking oil during a wave of persecution in pagan Rome. However, he was miraculously delivered from death, and then sentenced to the mines on the prison Island of Patmos where he wrote the prophetic book of Revelation. He was later freed and returned to serve as Bishop of Edesa (modern day Turkey). Record has him as the only apostle who died peacefully due to old age.

v) Peter: he was crucified upside down on an X-shape cross; he told his tormentors that he was unworthy to die in the same way as his Lord Jesus Christ died.

vi) James: he was the leader of the church in Jerusalem; he was thrown over a hundred feet down from the southeast pinnacle of the Temple when he refused to disown his faith in Christ. On discovering that he survived the fall, his tormentors beat him to death with a huge club; and this was the same pinnacle where Satan had taken Christ during temptation.

vii) James (son of Zebedee): a fisherman by trade when Jesus called him to a lifetime of ministry, he was beheaded at Jerusalem. The Roman officer who guarded him watched amazed as James defended his faith at his trial. Later, the officer walked besides him to the place of execution. Overcame by conviction, he declared his conversion to the judge and knelt besides James to accept beheading as well as a Christian.

viii) Nathaniel (aka Bartholomew): he was a missionary to Asia, and witnessed for our Lord in the present day Turkey. He was martyred for his preaching in Armenia where he was whipped to death.

> ix) Andrew: he was also crucified on an X-shaped cross in Patras, Greece; after being whipped severely by seven soldiers, they tied his body to the cross with ropes to prolong his agony. It is reported that when he was led toward the cross, Andrew saluted it with these words: "I've long desired and expected this happy hour. The cross has been consecrated by the body of Christ hanging on it." He continued preaching to his tormentors for two days until he died.
>
> x) Thomas: he was stabbed with a spear in India during one of his missionary trips to establish a church in the sub-continent.
>
> xi) Jude: he was killed with arrows after refusing to renounce his faith in Christ
>
> xii) Matthias: the apostle chosen to replace Judas Iscariot the traitor, he was stoned and then beheaded for his remaining firm to the testimony of Christ.
>
> xiii) Paul: he was tortured and then beheaded by the Roman Emperor Nero in Rome in AD 67. Records show that he endured a length imprisonment which allowed him to write his many epistles to the churches that were formed and established in the vast Roman Empire. These letters which taught many of the foundational doctrines of Christianity, and they form a large portion of the New Testament.

This text serves to remind us that our sufferings here are indeed minor compared to the intense persecution and cold cruelty faced by the apostles and disciples during their times for the sake of Christianity.

*(1) Tell me the old, old story of unseen things above,
Of Jesus and His glory, of Jesus and His love.
Tell me the story simply, as to a little child,
For I am weak and weary, and helpless and defiled.*

Chorus
*Tell me the old, old story, tell me the old, old story,
Tell me the old, old story, of Jesus and His love.*

*(2) Tell me the story slowly, that I may take it in,
That wonderful redemption, God's remedy for sin.
Tell me the story often, for I forget so soon;
The early dew of morning has passed away at noon.
Tell me the old, old story, tell me the old, old story,
Tell me the old, old story, of Jesus and His love.*

*(3) Tell me the story softly, with earnest tones and grave;
Remember I'm the sinner whom Jesus came to save.
Tell me the story always, if you would really be,
In any time of trouble, a comforter to me.
Tell me the old, old story, tell me the old, old story,
Tell me the old, old story, of Jesus and His love.*

*(4) Tell me the same old story when you have cause to fear
That this world's empty glory is costing me too dear.
Yes, and when that world's glory is dawning on my soul,
Tell me the old, old story: "Christ Jesus makes thee whole."
Tell me the old, old story, tell me the old, old story,
Tell me the old, old story, of Jesus and His love.*

20. HE LEADETH ME
(Annung'amya Kya Ssanyu)
CS 393

The author of this hymn gives the account of how he was led to write the words. And here is the story told by Joseph H. Gilmore (1834 - 1918). "As a young man who recently had been graduated from Brown University and Newton Theological Institution, I was supplying for a couple of Sundays the pulpit of the First Baptist Church in Philadelphia. At the midweek service, on the 26th of March, 1862, I set out to give the people an exposition of the Twenty-third Psalm, which I had given before on three or four occasions, but this time I did not get further than the words "He Leadeth Me." Those words took hold of me as they had never done before, and I saw them in a significance and wondrous beauty of which I had never dreamed. It was the darkest hour of the Civil War. I did not refer to that fact — that is, I don't think I did — but it may subconsciously have led me to realize that God's leadership is the one significant fact in human experience, that it makes no difference how we are led, or where we are led, so long as we are sure God is leading us. At the close of the meeting a few of us in the parlor of my host, good Deacon Wattson, kept on talking about the thought which I had emphasized; and then and there, on a blank page of the brief from which I had intended to speak, I pencilled the hymn, talking and writing at the same time, then handed it to my wife and thought no more about it. She sent it to The Watchman and Reflector, a paper published in Boston, where it was first printed. I did not know until 1865 that my hymn had been set to music by William B. Bradbury. I went to Rochester [New York] to preach as a candidate before the Second Baptist Church. Going into their chapel on arrival in the city, I picked up a hymnal to see what they were singing, and opened it at my own hymn, "He Leadeth Me."

This reminds me of John's writings in the gospel, "To him the doorkeeper opens, and the sheep hear his voice; and he calls his own sheep by name and leads them out." John 10:3

What an interesting way to find that your writing had been published and was being used to encourage believers. This is actually my prayer that my good Lord may use this (my) publication to bless as many people through mindful worship and singing of these hymns but also use these words as not only inspirational but above all a devotional in churches, institutions, households and personal lives. Amen!!

Andrew Singo in his book titled "In God's time", wrote about trusting God's leadership for our destination in which he admonished us to trust His leadership: in all details of our lives the same way Moses told Joshua (Joshua 1:7); in tough times as Paul exhorts us in Galatians 6:9. He further emphasizes that the bible is full of wisdom concerning the way God wants His people to, and on how to have relationships that are loving, supportive and long term; and there are guidelines at every stage of our lives and in all circumstances of our lives. He also warns us of the enemies of God's leadership such as: impatience; our past hurtful experiences; quitting; fear; and a host of others that distract us from His leadership.

> *(1) He leadeth me, O blessed thought!*
> *O words with heav'nly comfort fraught!*
> *Whate'er I do, where'er I be*
> *Still 'tis God's hand that leadeth me.*
>
> *Chorus*
> *He leadeth me, He leadeth me, By His own He leadeth me;*
> *His faithful follower I would be, For by His hand He leadeth me.*
>
> *(2) Sometimes mid scenes of deepest gloom,*
> *Sometimes where Eden's bowers bloom,*
> *By waters still, over troubled sea,*
> *Still 'tis His hand that leadeth me.*
>
> *(3) Lord, I would place my hand in Thine,*
> *Nor ever murmur nor repine;*
> *Content, whatever lot I see,*
> *Since 'tis my God that leadeth me.*
>
> *(4) And when my task on earth is done,*
> *When by Thy grace the vict'ry's won,*
> *E'en death's cold wave I will not flee,*
> *Since God through Jordan leadeth me.*

21. IS MY NAME WRITTEN THERE??
(Siyagala Bugagga)
CH 617

This issue concerned Mary Kidder years ago. Born as Mary Ann Pepper (1820-1905), it is said she was blinded in her teens, but slowly recovered her sight. We know little more about her, except that she had a gift for writing poetry. Mrs. Kidder penned about a thousand hymns, but only this one has remained in common use. In this song published in 1878, she asks the penetrating question, "Is My Name Written There?", meaning in the Book of Life. Being denied access to heaven is a much worse fate than not being admitted to a gala reception. But it will be the fate of many. The Apostle Paul states it briefly, "I declare to you the gospel .... That Christ died for our sins" (I Cor. 15:1, 3). When the Philippian jailer asked, "What must I do to be saved?" Paul answered without hesitation, "Believe on the Lord Jesus Christ, and you will be saved." (Acts 16:30-31). Is your name written there? Don't put off making that crucial decision. Tomorrow might be too late.

There is one book whose contents should concern us above all others. It is called "The Book of Life." That book is mentioned eight times in the New Testament. Once, it is called "the Lamb's Book of Life" - the book belonging to the Lamb of God, the Lord Jesus Christ (Rev. 21:27). Jesus speaks of the importance of having our names being "written in heaven" (Lk. 10:20). Paul speaks of "fellow workers, whose names are in the Book of Life" (Phil. 4:3). That it lists those who qualify to enter into the heavenly kingdom is made clear by the warning in Revelation: "Anyone not found written in the Book of Life was cast into the lake of fire" (Rev. 21:15). And, "There shall by no means enter it anything that defiles, or causes an abomination or a lie, but only those who are written in the Lamb's Book of Life" (Rev. 21:27).

A story is told of a gifted Soloist who was asked to sing at the wedding of a very wealthy couple. She was thrilled and honored to be part of this special day. She was especially excited because she and her husband were invited to the reception at one of the most elaborate locations in the city. It was a place that she would never have been able to afford to attend otherwise. Following the wedding, with great expectations, she and her husband came to the reception location, a restaurant high above the city skyline. When they arrived at the door, the receptionist asked for their names but their names weren't on the list. She replied, "but I was the soloist". The receptionist said that made no difference, their names weren't on the list. Then they were ushered to a freight elevator which took them back down to the main floor. On the way down the soloist remembered that the invitation included an RSVP which she had forgotten to return. Her name wasn't in the book, so she wasn't allowed to enter the reception gala. What a disappointment they could have faced!!

(1) Lord, I care not for riches, neither silver nor gold;
I would make sure of Heaven, I would enter the fold.
In the book of Thy kingdom, with its pages so fair,
Tell me, Jesus, my Savior, is my name written there?
Is my name written there,
On the page white and fair?
In the book of Thy kingdom,
Is my name written there?

(2) Lord, my sins they are many, like the sands of the sea,
But Thy blood, O my Savior, is sufficient for me;
For Thy promise is written, in bright letters that glow,
"Though your sins be as scarlet, I will make them like snow."

(3) Oh! that beautiful city, with its mansions of light,
With its glorified beings, in pure garments of white;
Where no evil thing cometh to despoil what is fair;
Where the angels are watching, yes, my name's written there.
Yes my name's written there,
On the page white and fair?
In the book of Thy kingdom,
Yes my name's written there?

22. WE HAVE HEARD A JOYFUL SOUND, JESUS SAVES!
(Wulira Eky'essanyu)
CH 637

Priscilla Jane Owens was a public school teacher in the city of Baltimore for 49 years. She was also much involved in the work of the Sunday School, and wrote most of her hymns for use there. "Jesus Saves" was written for a missionary service of the Union Square Methodist Church which she attended in 1882. Owens was so passionate about evangelism not only in her vicinity but global evangelism. That is why her song is among the very few songs that challenge us to deliberately go out and share the word with all people of different races, tongues, that it is only Jesus who saves us from our fallen human nature. Her hymn reminds us of our responsibility to share the message of salvation ... "spread the tidings all around ... bear the news to every land ... tell to sinners far and wide ... give the winds a mighty voice". The message is that Jesus alone saves. And what will be the eventual result of this vital message? Revelation 7:10, "Behold, a great multitude which no one could number, of all nations, tribes, peoples, and tongues, standing before the throne and before the Lamb ... and crying out with a loud voice, saying, "Salvation belongs to our God who sits on the throne, and to the Lamb!" Let us share the message of salvation and look forward to that glorious day when the saved gather around the throne and praise the Lamb!

Many people don't feel that they need the Gospel, deluding themselves that their wisdom is more relevant that the Bible. But the Bible is God's Word. It is inspired by God and it is truth! Jesus himself said in John 14:6 "I am the way, the truth, and the life. No man comes unto the Father but through me." There is only one way to eternal life in heaven and that is through Jesus. Acts 4:12 reminds us "Nor is there salvation in any other, for there is no other name under heaven given among men by which we must be saved." Psalm 3:8, "Salvation belongs to the Lord." We as believers are told to take this message to those all around us. Acts 13:47, "This is what the Lord told us to do: I have made you a light for the other nations, to show people all over the world the way to be saved.'" We will often meet resistance and ridicule as we share the message that Jesus saves. But we are reminded in Romans 1:16, "For I am not ashamed of the gospel of Christ, for it is the power of God to salvation for everyone who believes, for the Jew first and also for the Greek.

This reminds me of a popular story about a certain young man who had just finished his studies from a theological college and was sent on internship to a certain Anglican church where he would find a senior clergy/priest to orient him into ministry and offer him apprenticeship. The senior priest welcomed him and informed him that he would minister the following Sunday as a gesture of welcoming and integrating him into ministry, which the young minister happily accepted. Sunday came and soon his opportunity of ministering appeared; and on standing up to greet the congregation, he did all the nitty-gritty expected of him in their ministry as a preamble for the sermon. He then asked them a critical question, "Do you know what I'm going to preach about?", obviously very many responded with a "NO" yet some very few voices accidently said "Yes". This prompted him to make this very strong statement, "Let those who know share with/ tell those who don't know!" and then he bade them farewell and wished them a blessed week. This made the senior priest so furious and he scolded him for not showing the basic responsibility in life and ministry, then later ordered him to prepare to minister also the following Sunday. The week swiftly passed and Sunday came, again this young cleric was on the pulpit, and he did the same thing as the previous Sunday service, "Do you know what I'm going to talk about today?". Most congregants were totally confused (had it been you, what would you answer?) and wondering what the implication/ reaction of either a "Yes" or "No" would be, but all the same they were greatly divided in that a big number said "Yes" and another equally big portion answered "No" lest he dupes them as he had done in the previous Sunday service. He happily responded, "May the good and gracious Lord bless you enormously! Let those who know happily share with those who don't know!" This saw him send off the worshippers with God's blessings indicating that his sermon was done. Once again, the senior priest was grossly disappointed with him and strongly scolded him for putting their ministry into such a massive shame. (The story continues but………)

But in reality, that message is the package that we ought to take from Owen's song that let those who have knowledge about the saving power and grace of our loving Lord Jesus share it with those who don't know in every land and sea, on mountains since that is Christ's command. Be blessed as you happily take that testimony!

(1) We have heard the joyful sound:
Jesus saves! Jesus saves!
Spread the tidings all around:
Jesus saves! Jesus saves!
Bear the news to every land,
climb the mountains, cross the waves;
Onward! 'tis our Lord's command;
Jesus saves! Jesus saves!

(2) Waft it on the rolling tide:
Jesus saves! Jesus saves!
Tell to sinners far and wide:
Jesus saves! Jesus saves!
Sing, you islands of the sea;
echo back, you ocean caves;
Earth shall keep her jubilee:
Jesus saves! Jesus saves!

(3) Sing above the battle strife:
Jesus saves! Jesus saves!
By His death and endless life
Jesus saves! Jesus saves!
Shout it brightly through the gloom,
when the heart for mercy craves;
Sing in triumph o'er the tomb:
Jesus saves! Jesus saves!

(4) Give the winds a mighty voice:
Jesus saves! Jesus saves!
Let the nations now rejoice:
Jesus saves! Jesus saves!
Shout salvation full and free;
highest hills and deepest caves;
This our song of victory:
Jesus saves! Jesus saves!

23. GOD BE WITH YOU TILL WE MEET AGAIN
(Katonda Abeerenga Naawe)
A & M 489   CH 35

This benediction hymn was written and published in 1882, by the Reverend Jeremiah Eames Rankin, who was, at the time, pastor of the First Congregational Church of Washington D.C. The poem that Rankin originally wrote had eight stanzas, but today the first, second, fourth and seventh stanzas are all that are commonly sung. Mr. Rankin wrote the following account regarding his writing of "God Be With You": "Written as a Christian good-bye, it was called forth by no person or occasion, but was deliberately composed as a Christian hymn on the basis of the etymology of "good-bye," which is "God be with you." On consulting the dictionary for the definition of the word 'good-bye', and it was found to be a contraction of 'God be with ye'. Very soon the first verse was completed. William Gould Tomer disengaged in the Union Army during the Civil War and then became a public school teacher in New Jersey where he composed the music for this text upon Dr. Rankin's request. A few years before his death, when the late President Theodore Roosevelt was making a farewell visit in Memphis, Tenn., a great audience of three thousand people sang in his honor the well-loved strain, "God be with you till we meet again." It is a wonderful prayer that has helped and encouraged multitudes over the years. In fact it is a great prayer and testimony for your friends anytime, not just when you are parting. Maybe on reading this text, you could consider "praying" this for those whom you love. The chorus includes that powerful truth that those in God's family will be reunited again, if not here on earth, then definitely in heaven. "Till we meet, till we meet, Till we meet at Jesus' feet. God be with you till we meet again."

One secular musician sang that "Goodbye is the saddest word". Leaving good friends and Christian brothers and sisters can sometimes be very hard emotionally, especially if you may not see them again for a long time. This normally disturbs me whenever I visit my dear mum and dad, who incidentally live barely a kilometre from my home but as I propose to leave after a visit it is visible that we all don't love that moment. Besides, this bring back to my mind the fact that I've always been a beloved son to my mum, the day I resolved/ proposed to leave home ever in my life was filled with tears and pleas to make me have a change of mind if possible. You know, it is especially me who spent most of my time at home (all my schooling time as a day scholar), so when I was in my final year (undergraduate) I resolved to go and rent an apartment so as to begin planning for my independent life quite early as a real man. This proposal of a goodbye to my mum, basically, was such a nightmare and I can never forget that scenario.

As we separate, we just never know what a day/ lifetime may bring and whether or not we will meet again on this earth. And as we separate from our friends, we do so with the desire that God will go with us and with our friends. And He does so since he has promised never to leave us or forsake His children and He has never behaved that way. I've grown up listening to this song basically when the worship service is done and congregants take a blessed opportunity to wish each other God's protection, counsels, guidance, goodness, faithfulness and blessings to be with them till they meet again either in this mortal life or at Jesus' feet in eternity.

(1) God be with you till we meet again,
By His counsels guide, uphold you,
With His sheep securely fold you,
God be with you till we meet again.
Till we meet, till we meet,
Till we meet at Jesus' feet;
Till we meet, till we meet,
God be with you till we meet again.

(2) God be with you till we meet again,
'Neath His wings securely hide you,
Daily manna still provide you,
God be with you till we meet again.
Till we meet, till we meet,
Till we meet at Jesus' feet;
Till we meet, till we meet,
God be with you till we meet again.

(3) God be with you till we meet again,
When life's perils thick confound you,
Put His arms unfailing round you,
God be with you till we meet again.
Till we meet, till we meet,
Till we meet at Jesus' feet;
Till we meet, till we meet,
God be with you till we meet again.

(4) God be with you till we meet again,
Keep love's banner floating o'er you,
Smite death's threat'ning
wave before you,
God be with you till we meet again.
Till we meet, till we meet,
Till we meet at Jesus' feet;
Till we meet, till we meet,
God be with you till we meet again.

24. TIS LOVE THAT MAKES US HAPPY
   (Tukola Lwa Kwagala)
   CH 567

Frank E. Belden (1858 – 1945) was the eldest of five children born to Stephen and Sarah (Harmon) Belden, older sister of Ellen Harmon White. About 1876 he moved to California where he began to compose music. Because of health reasons he moved to Colorado where he met and married Harriet MacDearmon who was also talented in music. They returned to Battle Creek in the 1880's where he connected with the Adventist publishing work. He and Edwin Barnes served as music editors of the Hymns and Tunes which was released in 1886. Belden also collaborated with his cousin, J. Edson White, on several song books. A disagreement arose between Belden and the Review and Herald over the royalties from "Hymns and Tunes". It was reported that Belden was greedy and wanted the money. In reality the agreement with the General Conference in 1886 was for his share of the royalties to go to mission work. When the Review and Herald took over the copyright to the hymnal, Belden did not want his share to go to the publishing house. Disillusioned, he separated himself from church work, but it did not "forsake his allegiance to the church or to the Lord." Belden's ability in penning both music and poetry was often demonstrated by his writing a song to fit a sermon while it was still being delivered. He would take the preacher's text and by the end of the service have a song ready for performance. "Christ in Song" is Belden's most recognizable contribution to Seventh-day Adventist hymnody, though he wrote hundreds of other songs throughout his career. The 1985 Seventh-day Adventist hymnal includes twelve hymns and four tunes, more than any other Adventist contributor.

Belden separated from the SDA church in 1907; he felt that the

Review and Herald was not giving him his just royalties (payment) for his songs. Near the end of his work on Christ in Song, Belden had begun writing songs for the noted evangelist Billy Sunday, which were included in "Songs for the King's Business". Belden, in the year of his death (1945), had a meeting with ministers Kenneth H. Wood and Carlyle B. Haynes. They came hoping to pray with him and encourage him, but he refused.

Is it possible for religion to became a habit - where we know all the right answers to all the questions - but that is as deep as it goes? Only God knows the heart, but how I pray that we meet this talented brother in heaven! One would wonder such a significant contrast between the spiritual/ inspired content of his song(s) and how his life ended, which brings such a spiritual depression. This guy has the record of having been the author of the biggest number of hymns in Adventist hymnal, and among others these are: Blessed Lord, how much I need Thee!; The Lord's our Rock.; I will sing of Jesus' love.; Ask not to be excused!; We'll build on the Rock.; Hark! The voice of Jesus.; Sweet promise is given.; The judgment has set!; O there'll be joy!; We'll tarry by the Living Water.

This hymn can be connected to 2 Corinthians 5:14, "For the love of God constrains us; because we thus judge, that if one died for all, then were all dead." But also read Philippians 2:2-7, 14-15

This reminds me of a host of fallen and some still living Christians-turned-secular musicians who actually begun their musical career well in Christian music ministry but later got derailed due to a variety of reasons known to them. Among other were: late Kezia Nambi, late Martin Angume, Betty Mpologoma and her sister Nassolo, and the list is endless. Belden affirms that this world is full of sorrow, of sickness, death, and sin; but with loving heart we'll do our part and try some soul to win. He further adds that when this life is over, and we are called above, that our song shall be, eternally, of Jesus and His love. What a powerful message for us who live in the final days of earth's history!!!

This further reminds me of a remarkable statement that was made by Goldmeyer (a onetime Premier of Israel) that has concrete life lessons for us both as Christians who live in this unjust and painful world but also as citizens in a world that is so competitive, filled with both desperation and uncertainty about even the near future. Commenting on Israel's future that has so mingled in despair, he said

"Israel has many problems, what shall we do; we don't have oil, nor any mineral resource" but he concluded, "the only thing we have for survival is ATTITUDE".

The truth is that most Christian virtues are anchored on "faith", which is a synonym/ another name for: right attitude; confidence; trust; reliance; conviction; belief; devotion; loyalty; but above all "love". Hence, Paul's reference in 2 Timothy 1:7 "For God has not given us a spirit of fear, but of power and love and of a sound mind." And most importantly, 1 John 4:18 "There is no fear in love, but perfect love casts out fear, because fear involves torment. But he who fears has not been made perfect in love."

John's counsels are perfectly in harmony with this memorable statement: "**Courage is not the absence of fear, but rather the judgment that something else is more important than fear.**"

> 'Tis love that makes us happy,
> 'Tis love that smooths the way;
> It helps us mind, it makes us kind
> To others everyday
>
> **Chorus**

God is love; we're His little children.
God is love; we would be like Him.
'Tis love that makes us happy,
'Tis love that smooths the way;
It helps us "mind," it makes us kind
To others every day.

This world is full of sorrow,
Of sickness, death, and sin;
With loving heart we'll do our part,
And try some soul to win.

And when this life is over,
And we are called above
Our song shall be, eternally,
Of Jesus and His love.

25. GOD WILL TAKE CARE OF YOU
SDAH 99

Walter Stillman Martin was born March 8, 1862 in Rowley, Essex Co., Massachusetts. He attended Harvard University where he studied for the ministry, and was later ordained as a Baptist minister. His wife, Civilla Durfee Holden, was born August 21, 1866, in Jordan, Nova Scotia, Canada. They came together through a mutual interest in music. She had for years taught music before meeting Walter. With his musical talents, their lives together as a husband and wife team was a blessing to them, and ultimately to the world.

Civilla wrote texts for many of the hymns he produced including their very popular, "God Will Take Care of You." She explained the circumstances behind the writing of this now famous song. "I was confined to a sick bed in a Bible school in Lestershire, New York. My husband was spending several weeks at the school, making a songbook for the president of the school". One Sunday, Walter was to preach in a town some distance from the school. Since Civilla became unable to attend because of sickness, he wanted to cancel his trip. While it was being passionately discussed, their nine year old son said, "Father, don't you think that if God wants you to preach today, He will take care of Mother while you are away?" The old saying, "Out of the mouth of babes," comes to mind! Martin kept his appointment, and when he returned that evening, he found his wife greatly improved though he had been so nervous. Mrs. Martin had written a new hymn based on her son's faithful remark earlier that day, and within an hour, Mr. Martin wrote the melody. That very evening a couple of other teachers at the school came by, and they all sang the song together. Later in the week it was sung at one of the school assemblies, and the suggestion was made for it to be included in the new hymnbook. Thus, it was first published in 1905 in "Songs of Redemption," compiled by Martin and John A. Davis.

Memory text; 2 Corinthians 5:7 "For we walk by faith, not by sight."

This song is so beloved to me because, just like Martin and Civilla, my wife and I first met through music ministry and of course initially there was nothing we could see in each other but this opportunity brought a wealth of reasons that led to an enduring relationship. You know, there is a beauty in loving someone with whom you share a lot in common. The more we got involved in music ministry, the more closer and closer we got to each which we believe was God's design for our lives not until the remarkable day of Sunday 14th February 2010 (Valentine's Day) that the good Lord officiated at our wedding. What is so interesting is that some skills/ talents can be quite hereditary in nature; this is because our daughter embraced the talent at a very early stage in that by ten (10) month she could sing/ hum some rhythms clearly well that one time she was in a Taxi (Matatu) with the mum and on humming a popular song of "Baby Jesus, I love you!", passengers were filled with admiration owing to such a happening.

Besides, a much stronger reason as to why I adore this song is due to, one challenging day at Kyambogo University when I was pursuing my undergraduate studies I was so demoralized by the hell we were going through as SDA students in public universities. I had a backlog of missed exams that had been scheduled on Sabbath and we seemed not to be having a relief/ solace since around that time, our brethren at Makerere University had lost such a court case, and so everything appeared to be bad news. That day, unlike other days when I could only for lectures due to my busy working schedule, I happened to be on campus early enough so that I found myself attending the lunch time fellowship at the SDA church on campus. I vividly remember my brother, Waiswa Moses, brought a song I'd never heard in life and in my music career titled "God will take care of you!" and I was greatly soaked in a sea of thoughts and uncertainties but I was thrilled with the music and spiritual lessons in words. Since then, I've always referred to that song in time of hardships whenever I seem to be perplexed. May the good Lord bless as you also sing and contemplate over this song.

Be not dismayed whatever be tide, God will take care of you;
Beneath His wings of love abide, God will take care of you.

God will take care of you; thro' everyday, over all the way,
He will take care of you; God will take care of you

Thro' days of toil when heart doth fail, God will take of you;
When dangers fierce your path assail, God will take of you.

All you may need He will provide, God will take care of you;
Nothing you ask will be denied, God will take care of you.

No matter what may be the test, God will take care of you;
Lean, weary one up on His breast, God will take of you.

26. I SHALL KNOW HIM (when my life work is ended)
(Bwe Ndimala Olugendo Lwange)
CH 849

Globally, all music lovers have appreciated many of the over 8,000 hymns that were written by the blind author Fanny Crosby. When she was just six-weeks-old, Fanny got an infection that was made worse when a phony doctor poured hot poultice on her inflamed eyes. She became almost completely blind, only able to distinguish day from night.

But it is said that one woman on television proclaimed – Fanny's blindness stimulated other gifts and abilities. She had an incredible memory and was able to recite whole sections of the Bible, including the Pentateuch, the four Gospels, and all of Proverbs.

Perhaps it was her knowledge of the Word that comforted her in times of trouble. While many of us might view blindness as a disability, Fanny viewed it as a gift from God and even once said that if she could meet the man who caused it, she would tell him that he unwittingly did her "the greatest favor in the world."

Near the end of the nineteenth century, Fanny was visiting the Lake Chautauqua Institute, in Western New York State. In those days this was a place for Christian fellowship, great preaching, and singing of wonderful hymns. It was here that she met John R. Sweney. After a busy day at the camp meeting, both were taking a rest on the front porch of the grand hotel when John asked an interesting question of Fanny. "Fanny," he asked, "do you think we'll recognize our friends in heaven?" Initially her response was positive. She then added, "John, that's not what you really want to know. You wonder how an old lady who has been blind all her life could even recognize one person, let alone her Lord and Savior. Well I've given it a lot of thought and I don't think I'll have a problem. But if I do, when I get to heaven, I'm going to look around and when I see the one who I think is my Savior, I'm going to walk up to Him and say, 'May I see your hands?' When I see the nail prints in the hands of my Savior, then I'll know I've found my Jesus." "Oh Fanny," John said, "that would make a great song." "No thank you," she replied. "I'm tired, I'm going to bed". Well the next morning, bright and early, Fanny met John for breakfast and before they went their separate ways, she dictated the words of this great hymn. It is about heaven and the hope of each Christian should be to see our Lord, face to face. What a powerful message to us in this unpredictable life!!

Many folks take this hymn to be one dedicated to sorrowful events such as burial ceremonies, vigils, requiems but it can really be used in joyful moments to remind us of the reality of this volatile mortal life and also the fact that one day we shall see our Redeemer face by face. Crosby encourages us that above all, we ought to long to meet our Saviour first.

(1) When my life work is ended, and I cross the swelling tide,
When the bright and glorious morning I shall see
I shall know my Redeemer when I reach the other side,
And His smile will be the first to welcome me.

Chorus:
I shall know Him, I shall know Him
And redeemed by His side, I shall stand.
I shall know Him, I shall know Him,
By the print of the nails in His hand.

(2) Oh, the soul thrilling rapture when I view His blessed face
And the luster of His kindly beaming eye;
How my full heart will praise Him for the mercy, love, and grace
That prepared for me a mansion in the sky.

*(3) Oh, the dear ones in glory, how they beckon me to come,
And our parting at the river I recall;
To the sweet vales of Eden they will sing my welcome home,
But I long to meet my Saviour first of all.*

*(4) Thro' the gates of the city in a robe of spotless white,
He will lead me where no tears will ever fall;
In the glad song of ages I shall mingle with delight,
But I long to meet my Saviour first of all.*

27. WE KNOW NOT THE HOUR
(Simanyi Ekiseera)
CH 540

Franklin Edson Belden was by far the most prolific Adventist hymn writer of the 19th century. Born in 1858 - Died 1945. He was the first born of five children born to Ellen White's oldest sister Sarah and her husband Stephen Belden, In Battle Creek ,Michigan. To give some idea just how talented Belden was he could write a new song within an hour, while the preacher was reading the morning scripture, he would then slip out and write a new hymn based on the text which he and his new wife, Harriet MacDearmon 'a very fine singer' would stand and sing. After the service he would give a copy to the preacher. Frank was already writing hymns by the time he was in his early twenties. He wrote several hundred hymns during his lifetime.

In 1888 Frank Belden went to the General Conference session in Minneapolis. Unfortunately, he did not accept righteousness by faith there. Ellen White in Australia, wrote to her nephew to plead with him to accept and believe the doctrine of Righteousness by Faith. Once she wrote a 15 page letter to work on his Christian experience. It seem like he was making progress, but he soon slipped back.

While actively writing for the church, he compiled and assisted with others in the following hymnbooks: Hymns and Tunes 1886 - Joyful Greeting for the Sabbath School 1868 - Songs of Freedom 1891 - and Gospel Song Sheaf 1894. Probably the most popular hymnbook ever used in the SDA Church was his "Christ In Song" Book published in 1900 - revised and enlarged in 1908. A whole generation of Adventists used and loved this book of hymns.

"But of that day and hour no one knows, no not even the angels of heaven, but the Father only." Matthew 24:36; "Watch therefore, for you do not know what hour your Lord is coming". Matthew 24:42

This reminds of a story that one brother told regarding people over-anticipating Christ's return to the point of even setting date/ deadlines and practically resigning from the world. He is called Elder Mangeni Solomon, and was desirous of pursuing his Doctorate in an engineering related field but many Christians were discouraging him, arguing that when will he use/ profit from his PhD since Jesus is coming back very soon. One day, he shared it with one old man in the countryside, and this gentleman strongly motivated him to pursue his dream narrating to him his experience that, on the arrival of the Adventist message (news of Christ's imminent return), those who preached it to them were so eager (impulsive) to see their Savior's return. He tells that they reached a point that they advised believers to cut themselves off the worldly things like riches since they are only temporal and they might eclipse their spiritual wealth. This followed orders to destroy coffee and banana plantations in anticipation of heavenly riches which were really at hand. In short, these people destroyed their means of livelihood and shortly after, they went through a kind of desperation that is untold of, basically when their over-anticipation didn't bear results of Christ's return as they had projected. That is why this old man advised my brother to happily pursue his PhD since we know not the hour of our Master's appearing.

It further more reminds me of the fact that now, I would have been either an engineer or a medical doctor but when I was doing my O-level (1998 – 2001), such gospel that was looming in the Christian circle basically due to the craze of the year 2000 affected my career choices. Radical Christian brethren dissuaded some of us from having big future plans since, "Christ's return was at hand", and some of us were performing quite well in sciences but begun wondering whether they were worth the trouble, and after all it is almost wastage of valuable time. This saw many even drop from school and others lost the interest in serious studying. Of course, I don't really regret because later I realized that it was God's design that I pursue a career in Financial economics/ investment management but, as Christian we need to be cautious when it comes to setting dates for Christ's returning, like what has been happening in world history such as in year 1844 (the great disappointment), and the year 2000.

1. *We know not the hour of the Master's appearing;*
yet signs all fortell that the moment is nearing
When He shall return 'tis a promise most cheering
But we know not the hour.

Chorus
He will come, let us watch and be read-y
He will come, hallelujah! Hallelujah!
He will come, in the clouds of His Father's bright glory
But we know not the hour.

2. *There's light for the wise who are seeking salvation*
There's truth in the book of the Lord's revelation;
Each prophecy points to the great consummation
But we know not the hour.

3. *We'll watch and we'll pray, with our lamps trimmed and burning*
We'll work and we'll wait till the Masters returning;
We'll sing and rejoice, every omen discerning
But we know not the hour.

28. STAND UP FOR JESUS
(Wesibe Kulwa Yesu)
A & M 307   CH 354

During 1857–58, revival broke out in Philadelphia, P.A. (I love the name Philadelphia because of its meaning "brotherly love" but also the name of my church family is called Philadelphia). A young preacher called Dudley Tyng, one day preached to 5000 men using Exodus 10:11 as his text, "Go now ye that are men and serve the Lord", and about 1000 responded to his invitation that evening by giving their lives to Christ and serve Him as Dudley had impressed it on them. On the following Wednesday, Dudley had resolved to go to his countryside home so as to relax from the long period preaching. As he was out checking his corn-shelling machine, his arm accidentally got pulled into the machine and was cut off. The doctors didn't believe he would live but they would console his fellow ministers who had served with him in the evangelistic crusades that Dudley would get well. While he lay in great pain, he entreated his doctors to accept Christ with a room filled with other preachers whom he asked to sing aloud, "can you not sing, men??" Of course, it was so devastating for his fellow preachers that stood in shock and could hardly sing. His last admonition to his friends was to, "Tell the people to stand up for Jesus". That regardless of the life circumstances, we all ought to stand up for Jesus and lift His banner up not forgetting that the battle could be hard but we should not fear because Christ is with us the Lord of hosts and the Eternal commander.

George Duffield witnessed his friend's death that day and heard his dying words. That week he used his fallen friends' words to compose the hymn, "Stand up, Stand up for Jesus!"

The scriptural reading comes from Proverbs 27:17, "Iron sharpens iron; so a man sharpens his fellow man." There is sound reason why Duffield chose to refer to men because God from creation charged them with the responsibility of being the head of everything beginning with the household to other crucial managerial responsibilities both in church and the secular world. That is why as a build-up to the fact, I have chosen to share with you ten (10) features or unspoken needs of real Christian men that I used as a sermon on one Adventist Men's Sabbath, which I believe blessed the life of those who fellowshipped that Sabbath:

> 1. Men need Action; this is because men's self-image is largely determined by what they do and accomplish – with solid and tangible result both for their households, church, community and the country at large.
>
> 2. Men need Safety; there is one common rule for males, "Thou shall not show emotions". It would be very unbecoming of a man to display emotion since men are expected to have higher levels of self control and be in position to encourage others but not: crying, being extremely happy, and showing fear and anxiety, among other emotional tendencies.
>
> 3. Men need to be challenged; this is because from school time there are challenges with final exams, in the business world there is a challenge with a big sale or take-over/ new venture. Men grow up with such and a lot more challenges, that is why even Christ was not exceptional since He loved it but he could also challenge others like scribes, Sadducees and Pharisees.

4. Men need to get to the point; they normally want to know what the program is all about but not to take time on fluff (lots of details that are not worth listening to). They don't entertain stories and beating around the bush but are so desirous of getting to the real point of the matter.

5. Men need to Win; men grow up with pressure to win (Galatians 6:3-5). They are taught to be independent and self-sufficient in everything they purpose to do and they are groomed not to have failure as an option in all aspects of life – marriage, business, ministry, leadership, etc.

6. Men need to Dream; parents and educators ought to train men to grow up dreaming and scheming big so as to have concrete and sustainable achievement that would boost their profiles and self-esteem.

7. Men need other men like them. They ought to be in company of men just like them so as to share their big dreams but also their fears and weaknesses.

8. Men need help working around daily work; men and their families are continually getting worn out by take-overs and cut throat competition. This, coupled with emotional weariness of long and odd hours men work, compounds their already tiresome and monotonous life due to lack of time on them.

9. Men need Healing; many a men hardly receive gratitude from their children, wives and bosses for the great job they do. They normally get discouraged and desperate to the extent that they really need refuge to heal from such desperation basically from their dear wives and children.

10. *The need to Identify; males should be taught to identify themselves with other men who cherish the Adventist message (that of Christ's soon return to end the reign of evil that is rampant in this spoilt generation).*

Stand up! Stand up for Jesus! Ye soldiers of the cross,
Lift high His royal banner, It must not suffer loss;
From victory unto victory, His army shall He lead,
Till every foe is vanquished, And Christ is Lord indeed.

Stand up! Stand up for Jesus! The trumpet calls obey;
Forth to the mighty conflict, in this His glorious day,
Ye that are His now serve Him, against unnumbered foes;
Let courage rise with danger, and strength to strength oppose.

Stand up! Stand up for Jesus! Stand in His strength alone;
The arm of flesh will fail you; you dare not trust your own,
Put on the gospel armour, and watching unto prayer,
Where duty calls, or danger, Be never wanting there.

Stand up! Stand up for Jesus! The strife will not be long;
This day the noise of battle, The next the victor's song,
To him that overcomes, A crown of life shall be;
He with the king of glory, shall reign eternally.

29. LOVE DIVINE, ALL LOVES EXCELLING
(Kwagala Kwo Ayi Mukama)
A & M 205   CH 142

Charles Wesley wrote something like six thousand hymns during his lifetime. He spent much of his life on horseback travelling from church to church, so you might wonder how he accomplished this. A part of the answer is found in the fact that he was naturally gifted -- poetry welled up in him, allowing him to express his deep faith through hymns. Another part of the answer is that he organized himself for his task. He developed a kind of shorthand so that he could quickly jot down ideas as they came to him. He carried note cards in his pocket so that he could record his thoughts even while riding a horse. When he reached his destination, he would transform his rough notes into finished verse.

"Love Divine, All Loves Excelling" is one of Charles Wesley's greatest hymns (1707-88), first published in 1747 in his brother John Wesley's collection. He was a prolific hymn writer of the 18th century. Coming from a musical family, he left a lasting legacy of congregational song. The youngest of 18 children, Charles possessed prodigious talents that soon blossomed. Little did he know that "Love Divine, All Loves Excelling," would rise to become one of the most popular and consistently vocalized Christian songs. Writing hymn texts that are solidly based on the Scriptures gives them an appeal across denominational lines. It is estimated that during his lifetime, Wesley penned more than 9,000 poems of a spiritual nature, 6,000 of which are hymns. His writings were passionate and well-crafted, conveying the true essence of Christian teaching. A substantial number of his writings were completed while riding on horseback to his evangelical meetings. What really set Charles apart from other hymn writers was his effective use of scriptural allusions, providing a spiritual roadmap whereby individuals could imagine a Christ-centred life.

Scholars suggest that he was able to compose about 10 lines of verse daily for 50 years. Charles' brother John sometimes served as editor to his hymns. John's typical response was "some were good, some were mediocre, and some were exceptional." John can also be credited with improving the singability of Charles' hymns. Both John and Charles were instrumental in changing the spiritual environment of Britain during the 18th century. In doing so, they formed the bedrock of what Methodism has become worldwide. Their unwavering devotion to expressing Christian spirituality through hymns has impacted individuals across all denominational lines.

Wesley married Sara Gwynne in 1749. She was a constant companion to him on his evangelical journeys. Only five of their eight children survived infancy. Charles Wesley Jr. (1757-1834) and Samuel Wesley (1766-1837) were musical like their father, and his daughter Sarah (1759-1828) was gifted in spiritual poetry.

The hymn is really a prayer -- a prayer to Jesus, who is "Love Divine, All Loves Excelling." It invites Jesus to make his dwelling in us -- to visit us with his salvation -- to enter our hearts. It invites him to take away our love of sinning -- to set our hearts at liberty. It concludes by asking Jesus to finish his new creation (we are his new creation) so that we might be pure and spotless -- perfectly restored -- ready for heaven.

Like many hymns, Love Divine is loosely Trinitarian in organization: Christ is invoked in the first stanza as the expression of divine love; the Holy Spirit in the second stanza as the agent of sanctification;

the Father in the third stanza as the source of life; and the Trinity (presumably) in the final stanza as the joint Creator of the New Creation. Like many hymns, too, this one is a tissue of Biblical quotations, including "Alpha and Omega" (st. 2) as an epithet of Christ, from Revelation 21:6; the casting of crowns before God's throne (st. 4), from Revelation 4:10; the promise that Christians shall be "changed from glory into glory" (st. 2 and 4), from 2 Corinthians 3:18; as well as other, more general allusions.

We are fortunate to be the recipients of the poetic genius of Charles Wesley. He influenced Methodism more than any other hymn writer. Upon hearing of Charles' death, an elderly Londoner asked, "Who will write poetry for us now?" What better way to be thought of, than by your poetic and spiritual impact on congregational song?

How I wish that as you sing this hymn, you keep in mind that it is a prayer in which you are asking God to dwell in you; to visit you with his salvation; and to enter your heart.

(1) Love divine, all loves excelling,
Joy of heaven, to earth come down,
Fix in us Thy humble dwelling,
All Thy faithful mercies crown.
Jesus, thou art all compassion,
Pure, unbounded love thou art;
Visit us with Thy salvation,
Enter every trembling heart.

(2) Breathe, O breathe
Thy loving Spirit
Into ev'ry troubled breast;
Let us all in Thee inherit;
Let us find the promised rest;
Take away the love of sinning,
Take our load of guilt away;
End the work of Thy beginning,
Bring us to eternal day.

(3) Come, almighty to deliver,
Let us all thy life receive;
Suddenly return, and never,
Never more thy temples leave.
Thee we would be alway blessing,
Serve Thee as Thy hosts above,
Pray, and praise Thee without ceasing,
Glory in Thy perfect love.

(4) Finish then Thy new creation;
Pure and spotless let us be;
Let us see Thy great salvation
Perfectly restored in Thee:
Changed from glory into glory,
Till in heaven we take our place,
Till we cast our crowns before Thee,
Lost in wonder, love and praise.

30. HOW GREAT THOU ART

The writing of the hymn and its verses was actually influenced by two thunderstorms. A young minister's two-mile walk in the rain provided the original inspiration for "How Great Thou Art." The Reverend Carl Boberg of Monsteras, on the southeast coast of Sweden, was 25 years old when he wrote the lyrics of this song after trekking through a thunderstorm from a church meeting two miles away. It was first published in 1886, under the title "O Store Gud". Boberg wrote a poem, not meaning to write a hymn, but later heard it being sung to an old Swedish tune. More than forty years later, an English missionary, Stuart Hine, first heard the song in Russia. He and his young wife were missionaries to the Carpathian area of Russia, then a part of Czechoslovakia. There, they heard a very meaningful hymn that was a Russian translation of Carl Boberg's "O Store Gud" (O Great God). While ministering in the Carpathian Mountains, Hine found himself in the midst of a threatening storm. The thunder, as it rolled through the mountain range, was so awesome that it reminded Hine of the beautiful Russian hymn that had already become so dear to him. English verses began to form in his mind, verses that were suggested by portions of the Russian translation. He actually added the final verse.

This hymn was even once voted as America's favorite hymn. Although it had its origin in Europe, it still was not widely known until 1957, when the Billy Graham Crusade in New York City, with the singing of George Beverly Shea, launched it around the world. It was performed nearly a hundred times during those meetings and countless times ever since. I love the references in it to creation, to salvation and especially to the coming of Christ. What a triumphant final verse. As I sing this majestic hymn of praise and adoration, I can't help realizing anew the omnipotence of the Creator who did it all.

Carl asserts that: when through the woods and forest glades I wander; and hear the birds sing sweetly in the trees; when I look down, from lofty mountain grandeur; and see the brook, and feel the gentle breeze. This reminds me a story about David, the shepherd, written by Gerald Wheeler in his publication titled, "Beyond Life." It states that, "Centuries ago a shepherd gazed up at the desert night sky. As the stars burned in the blackness, outlining the darker smudge of the distant mountains of Moab, their grandeur and distance seared a sense of awe in his mind. The sky was so vast, and he was so small. Unbidden, a question came to his lips; one he wanted to suddenly ask God. 'When I look at your heavens, the work of your fingers, the moon and the stars that you have established; what are human beings that you are mindful of them, mortals that you care for them?' (Psalms 8:3-)

There is a story on nature that talks about the life of an eagle and the lessons we can draw from such a wonderful life:

The eagle can live up to 70 years; but to do this, it must make a hard decision. In its 40th year, its long and flexible talons (nails) can no longer grab prey which serves as food; its long and sharp beak becomes bent; the feathers become old, thick and heavy. These thick and heavy feathers stick to its chest and make it difficult to fly. Then the eagle is left with two options: DIE or go through a painful process of CHANGE. The process requires that the flies to a mountain top and sit on its nest; then it knocks its beak against a rock until it plucks it out. Then it will wait for a new beak to grow back, which it will use to pluck off the old talons. When its new talons grow again, it starts plucking its old-aged feathers: this is change that is worth sustaining the pain. And after this, the eagle takes its famous flight of rebirth and lives for another 30 more years.

Change is needed in life so as to:

To survive and live; we, too, have to start the change process by plucking out our unpleasant memories, negative habits, and fixed mindsets.

Only freed from the past burdens can we take advantage of the present opportunities that our good Lord avails us.

In order to take a new journey ahead in the future, one ought to let go of his negative old-limiting beliefs.

We should open up our fixed mindsets so as to be able to fly again like an eagle.

(1) O Lord my God, When I in awesome wonder,
Consider all the worlds Thy Hands have made;
I see the stars, I hear the rolling thunder,
Thy power throughout the universe displayed.

Chorus

Then sings my soul, My Saviour God, to Thee,
How great Thou art, How great Thou art.
Then sings my soul, My Saviour God, to Thee,
How great Thou art, How great Thou art!

(2) When through the woords, and
forest glades I wander,
And hear the birds sing sweetly in the trees.
When I look down, from lofty mountain grandeur
And see the brook, and feel the gentle breeze

(3) And when I think, that
God, His Son not sparing;
Sent Him to die, I scarce can take it in;
That on the Cross, my
burden gladly bearing,
He bled and died to take away my sin.

(4) When Christ shall come,
with shout of acclamation,
And take me home, what
joy shall fill my heart.
Then I shall bow, in humble adoration,
And then proclaim: "My God,
how great Thou art!"

31. THE OLD RUGGED CROSS

During the early years of his ministry, Rev. George Bennard was "praying for a full understanding of the cross and its plan in Christianity."

Consequently, he spent many hours in study, prayer and meditation, until he could say, "I saw the Christ of the cross as if I were seeing John 3:16 leave the printed page, take form and act out the meaning of redemption."

During these days the theme of what was to be his most successful song came to him. He was staying in the Methodist church house at Pokagon, Michigan, while engaged in series of service in the Pokagon Church when he finally perfected his song and wrote down the words and music.

The song became immediately popular. Introduced before a large convention in Chicago, its fame spread rapidly throughout the Christian world.

Today, a twelve-foot high wooden cross stands on a roadside near Reed City, Michigan, honoring the composer. On it are the words 'Old Rugged Cross." A sign reminds passersby that this is the "Home of Living Author, Rev. Geo. Bennard."

Memory Text; Galatians 6:14 "But God forbid that I should glory except in the cross of our Lord Jesus Christ, by whom the world has been crucified to me, and I to the World."

Bennard's choice of vocabulary of the cross is so captivating, "On that old rugged cross, so despised by the world; has a wondrous attraction for me; for the dear Lamb of God left His glory above so as to bear it to dark Calvary." This takes me back to Paul's message to the Corinthian church but also to today's church that has almost completely lost the significance and honorable position of the cross of Jesus in their worship, having replaced it with a host of irrelevant worldly things. 1 Corinthians 1:18 "For the message of the cross is foolishness to those who are perishing, but to us who are being saved it is the power of God."

This song reminds me of a Christian man called Arthur Blessit, who for loving his Lord and being passionate about sharing the gospel, he has broken a couple of world records: travelling the longest distances for an around the world pilgrimage of 64,752 Km (40,235 miles), he began walking on 25th December 1969. This gentleman has trekked on all the seven continents including Antarctica; more than 321 countries carrying a wooden cross of Jesus (3.7 m / 12 ft long) all through for at least 46 years; he has been arrested on the way at least hundreds of times; he has traversed forests and lands of hostile, uncivilised and cannibalistic communities; he has spent days and nights without food; he has applauded by many for his heroic acts but equally despised by many for what they term as "madness" of the highest degree. But in all, he is trying to draw people's attention towards the One who was crucified on the cross and the significance of His crucifixion to the human race. By the way, to bring more clarity and background to the cross, the world through various cultures and countries has had a diversity of ways that they have been exercising their death penalty. But the cross was the Roman's crudest manner of punishing hard-core criminals so as to forcefully send messages to the rest of the community.

On the contrary, Christ reminds us: in Luke 9:23, 24 "If anyone desires to come after Me, let him deny himself, and take up his cross daily and follow me. For whoever desires to save his life will lose it, but whoever loses his life for My sake will save it." Mat. 10:38 "And he who does not take his cross and follow after Me is not worth of Me."

(1) On a hill far away stood an old rugged cross,
The emblem of suff'ring and shame;
And I love that old cross where the dearest and best
For a world of lost sinners was slain.

Chorus
So I'll cherish the old rugged cross,
Till my trophies at last I lay down;
I will cling to the old rugged cross,
And exchange it some day for a crown.

2 On that old rugged cross, so despised by the world,
Has a wondrous attraction for me;
For the dear Lamb of God left His glory above,
To bear it to dark Calvary.

3 In that old rugged cross, stained with blood so divine,
A wondrous beauty I see;
For 'twas on that old cross Jesus suffered and died,
To pardon and sanctify me.

4 To the old rugged cross I will ever be true,
Its shame and reproach gladly bear;
Then He'll call me some day to my home far away,
Where His glory for ever I'll share.

32. RESCUE THE PERISHING
(Wonya Bonna Abo Abali Mu Kibi)
CH 623

Fanny Crosby was sixty years old when she visited Chicago's Bowery Mission for the first time in 1880. She little dreamed that it would provide the inspiration for one of her most popular religious poems.

In days when reaching the lost seemed to be more of a priority for most believers, many hymn writers and evangelists would use the sea to illustrate the sin in which the lost were drowning. They would then refer to things, such as lighthouses and lifelines, as the Gospel which was needed to rescue drowning mankind. Such was the case with the prolific blind hymn writer, Fanny Crosby, who penned the words to "Rescue The Perishing". Fanny Crosby wrote this song and here she shares with us what prompted her to pen this beautiful hymn. "It was written in the year 1869, when I was forty-nine years old. Many of my hymns were written after experiences in New York mission work. This one was thus written. I was addressing a large company of working men one hot summer evening, when the thought kept forcing itself on my mind that some mother's boy must be rescued that night or not at all. So I made a pressing plea that if there was a boy present who had wandered from his mother's home and teaching, he would come to me at the close of the service. A young man of eighteen came forward and said, 'Did you mean me? I promised my mother to meet her in heaven, but as I am now living that will be impossible.' We prayed for him and he finally arose with a new light in his eyes and exclaimed in triumph, 'Now I can meet my mother in heaven, for I have found God!' A few days before, Mr. Doane, the musical composer, had sent me the subject, 'Rescue the Perishing,' and while I sat there that evening, the line came to me, 'Rescue the Perishing, care for the dying.' I could think of nothing else that night. When I arrived home I went to work on the hymn at once, and before I retired it was ready for the melody. The next day my song was written out and forwarded to Mr. Doane, who wrote the beautiful and touching music as it now stands to my hymn. In November, 1903, I went to Lynn, Massachusetts, to speak before the Young Men's Christian Association. I told them the incident that led me to write 'Rescue the Perishing,' as I have just related it. After the meeting a large number of men shook hands with me, and among them was a man, who seemed to be deeply moved. You may imagine my surprise when he said, 'Miss Crosby, I was the boy, who told you more than thirty-five years ago that I had wandered from my mother's God. The evening that you spoke at the mission I sought and found peace, and I have tried to live a consistent Christian life ever since. If we never meet again on earth, we will meet up yonder.'

As the man said this, he raised Crosby's hand to his lips; and before she had recovered from her surprise the man had gone; and remains to this day a nameless friend, who touched a deep chord of sympathy in Crosby's heart. Times have changed, but mankind is still drowning in the sea of sin. The Gospel has not changed and it can still rescue and save mankind, those who are drowning and headed for spiritual death. It must still be our desire and goal to share the Gospel which alone can rescue them. How I pray that everyone does his/ her part to rescue the perishing, with a renewed spirit.

This story rhymes well with Acts 13:47, "For the Lord gave us this command when he said, 'I have made you a light to the Gentiles, to bring salvation to the furthest corners of the earth." God has planned for Israel to be His light; through Israel came Jesus the light of the nations. This light would spread out and enlighten the whole world in a bid to rescue His people from perishing and also care for the dying at the hand of the devil.

(1) Rescue the perishing,
Care for the dying,
Snatch them in pity from sin and the grave;
Weep o'er the erring one,
Lift up the fallen,
Tell them of Jesus the Mighty to save.

Chorus
Rescue the perishing,
Care for the dying;
Jesus is merciful, Jesus will save.

(2) Though they are slighting Him
Still He is waiting,
Waiting the penitent child to receive;
Plead with them earnestly,
Plead with them gently:
He will forgive if they truly believe.

(3) Down in the human heart,
Crushed by the tempter,
Feelings lie buried that grace can restore;
Touched by a loving hand,
Wakened by kindness,
Chords that were broken will
vibrate once more.

(4) Rescue the perishing,
Duty demands it;
Strength for thy labor the Lord will provide;
Back to the narrow way
Patiently win them;
Tell the poor wand'rer a Savior has died.

33. COME THOU FOUNT OF EVERY BLESSING
(Jangu Yesu Obe Mu Nze)
CH 291

Robert Robinson (1735-1790) was eight years old at the time of his father's death. He was a very bright, headstrong boy who became increasingly more difficult for his mother to handle. When Robert turned 14, she sent him to London for an apprenticeship with a barber. Robert proceeded to get into even more trouble, taking on a life of drinking and gambling. At 17, Robert and some of his drinking buddies decided to attend an evangelistic meeting, with a plan to make fun of the proceedings. When George Whitfield began to preach, Robert felt as if the sermon was just for him. He did not respond to the altar call that night, but the words of the evangelist would haunt him for the next three years.

On Dec. 10, 1755, at age 20, Robert finally yielded his life to Christ, and very soon thereafter answered a call to the ministry. Three years later, as he was preparing to preach a sermon at the Calvinist Methodist Chapel in Norfolk, England, Robert wrote *Come Thou Fount of Every Blessing* to complement his sermon. The music for the hymn was composed by Asahel Nettleton in 1813.

Robert's situation fits so well in David's dilemma as recorded in Psalms 51:7-12, "Purify me from my sins, and I will be clean; wash me, and I will be whiter than snow. Oh, give me back my joy again; you have broken me- now let me rejoice. Don't keep looking at my sins. Remove the stain of my guilt. Create in me a clean heart, O God. Renew a loyal spirit within me. Do not banish me from your presence, and don't take your Holy Spirit from me. Restore to me the joy of your salvation, and make me willing to obey you." Because we are born sinners, our natural inclination is to please ourselves rather than God. David followed that inclination when he took another man's wife. We also ought to ask God to cleanse us from within, filling our hearts and spirits with new thoughts and desires. Right conduct can come only from a clean heart and spirit. Do you ever feel stagnant in your faith, as though you are just going through the motions? Has sin ever created a rift between you and God, and making God seem distant? God wants to be close to us so that we feel the joy of His salvation. Sin that is unconfessed makes our intimacy with God impossible. Confess your sins to God; you may still have to face some earthly consequences as David did, but God will give back the joy of your relationship with Him.

This hymn's story reminds me of a popular story of one Christian household that had a prayerful lifestyle in that they would always seek God's favor and protective grace before going to bed. One night, after having fellowshipped with their God, they prayed for those who are in sorrow and particularly those evil doers who hurt others due to the desperation they are facing in life as a result of hardships in life so that God can give them His grace, forgiveness and providence. The household later went to bed but little did they know that their door was left open, and also that as they were praying, assailants were just outside waiting for the opportune time to enter both to rob and destroy life. No sooner had they gone to bed than the attackers entered the house to achieve their agenda. On the contrary, as they entered, they felt being over powered by the goodness and heaviness of the prayer package that was addressed to them which was so self-less. Finally, they yielded to the pleading voice of the Holy Ghost that they had to replace their machete with the bible they found near the television set, arguing that they ought to take this spiritual instrument that has rendered these people's hearts so pure and full of self-sacrifice.

Months later, one man came to the church where this Christian household usually congregated for worship and later testified on when their plans to robe from a Christian household saved their lives and rescued their perishing soul. They commended that household's prayerful and self-less life that brought them back into Christ's fold and now they are happy and free in Jesus.

Just like these assailants and Robert, we can also call upon Christ to come, Him the fount of every blessing, to tune our hearts to sing His grace and be guided by His goodness in all ways of our life.

Come, Thou Fount of Every Blessing

Come, Thou Fount of every blessing,
Tune my heart to sing Thy grace;
Streams of mercy, never ceasing,
Call for songs of loudest praise.
Teach me some melodious sonnet,
Sung by flaming tongues above.
Praise the mount! I'm fixed upon it,
Mount of Thy redeeming love.

34. NEAR TO THE HEART OF GOD

Cleland Boyd McAfee (1866 – 1944) an American theologian and Presbyterian minister wrote these words in 1903. But like so many of the great hymns, it was born out of tragic circumstances. At that time McAfee was preacher and choir director of the campus Presbyterian Church at Park College, Parkville, Mo.

To be creative, Rev. McAffee prepared an original hymn for his church choir each quarter during the Holy Communion.

He usually wrote his stanzas on the theme he chose for his sermon, setting them to appropriate music.

His people began to anticipate their gifted minister's hymns and tunes with the same eagerness with which they looked forward to his sermons.

Then that tragedy struck with unexplained suddenness. Diphtheria claimed his brother's two precious daughters as victims. The brothers and sister, with their close-knit families, offered to the bereaved parents all the love and understanding and sympathy their hearts could muster

The young pastor began to think about the communion hymn he wanted to write for the following Sunday morning. Soon he was saying to himself, "We can find peace and comfort if we stay near to the heart of God".

And soon the words were flowing from his facile pen, and he found himself writing, *"There is a place of quiet rest, Near to the heart of God; A place where sin cannot molest, Near to the heart of God."*

His daughter described the account in her book, "Near to the Heart of God". Hymnologist William J. Reynolds quotes the account: "The family and town were stricken with grief. My father often told us how he sat long and late thinking of what could be said in word and song on the coming Sunday. So he wrote the little song. The choir learned it at the regular Saturday night rehearsal, and afterward they went to Howard McAfee's home and sang it as they stood under the sky outside the darkened, quarantined house. It was sung again on Sunday morning at the communion service. And in the years since, it has been a real comfort to many of us who have learned that we need to "draw nigh" to the blest Redeemer, sent from the heart of God, who is always there to comfort us and cheer us and guide us.

People have always wished to meet their God in a place of quietness so as to privately and silently fellowship with Him without any interference. This has seen some seek for mountains (like my home is near a popular Pentecostal church called "Prayer Mountain" an exclusive place at the top of the hill). Others resolve to go to the shores of water bodies, and others in caves where no one else except the worshippers can reach. But the reality is despite these places being rather exclusive to some or even many would-be distracters, they are still situated in a sinful world where sin can reach the worshippers and molest them. That is why some reports that emerge later indicate a lot of promiscuity, theft and sexual pervasive activities in such "holy places". But: there is a unique "place of quiet rest, near to the heart of God", and it is "a place where sin cannot molest, near to the heart of God". MacAfee further argues that there is a place of comfort sweet, near to the heart of God; a place where we and our Savior meet, near to the heart of God. Maybe the events of your life are pressing you for that help. Then draw nigh to Him and He will draw nigh to you. He is always there to meet you when you seek Him.

> 1 *There is a place of quiet rest,*
> *Near to the heart of God,*
> *A place where sin cannot molest,*
> *Near to the heart of God.*

35. HOW FIRM A FOUNDATION
(Omusingi Gwaffe Munywevu)
CH 255

The authorship of this hymn is one of those that is filled with controversy despite the hymn's popularity world over. On the contrary, some studies suggest that it was authored by R. Keene who was once a song leader in Dr. Rippon's church in the mid 18th Century. As I've highlighted that despite the looming controversy over its real authorship, the words have been an inspiration to many across generations up to the present basically because it reminds us of the only true, solid Foundation for our lives and that is none other than the glorious Lord, Jesus Christ. For over two centuries this hymn has been a favorite and solid reminder for many. It was General Robert E. Lee's favorite hymn and was included in his funeral service as it was in the funerals of American presidents Theodore Roosevelt and Woodrow Wilson. President Andrew Jackson called for it to be sung on his deathbed. On Christmas Eve 1898, American units involved in the Spanish-American War joined together to sing the hymn that is the units were from the North and the South. It was first published in 1787 in Dr. John Rippon's Selection of Hymns and for many years people thought he had written it although for him, he attributed the authorship simply to "K--" which many a hymn enthusiasts believe was R. Keene.

In Matthew 7:23-27, Jesus gives the illustration of the wise man who built his house on the rock, a sure foundation, and when the storms came the house on the rock stood firm. But the foolish man built his house upon the shifting sands and when the storm came it collapsed.

Today we live in a society where many deny that there are any absolutes in life and this is at times referred to as "relativism" or making every truth/ fact/ realities to be relative according to subjective judgment of whoever cares. People just do what they think is right in their own eyes and they build their lives on the shifting sand that is premised on their judgments. And when the storms arise they have no hope for today or tomorrow. Too many reject the firm foundation of the absolutes and truth revealed to us in the Bible which has led to their swift destruction since they disregard one standing reality in life that states that the fear of the Lord leads to a longer life span. This can be explained in the way that our good Lord inspires us to make rational decisions in our daily living simply because we are anchored on a firm Foundation

This reminds us of the need to make the truth of the Scriptures our firm foundation of the Christian life. The verses reflect the application of Scripture to our lives. In verse two we are reminded of His presence and His promise to strengthen us and uphold us. It echoes Isaiah 41:10. Verse three reminds us of His presence when we walk through the deep waters which will come our way. Verse four reminds us of the fiery trials in which He will protect us and refine us. These verses reflect Isaiah 43:2. The final verse is a commitment to rest upon the Lord despite all the critics who will try to convince us otherwise and take away our victory. May the teachings and truth and absolutes of the Bible, God's guidebook to us, be the firm foundation that we built our lives upon. Matthew 7:25, ":And the rain descended, and the floods came, and the winds blew, and beat upon the house; and it fell not: for it was founded upon a rock."

> *Eagles fly alone and at high altitudes; they don't fly with sparrows or other small birds. This implies that one ought to keep good company (friends) that are incremental.*

Eagles have a strong vision; they are able to see far, and have the ability to visualize and make prompt decisions. One ought to quick at making rational decisions given the dynamic world in which we live.

Eagles don't eat dead things; they always feed on fresh prey. One should never rely on past success but keep looking for new frontiers to conquer and prove one's resourcefulness.

Eagles love the storm; the storm assures that the eagle will soar high. One must face challenges knowing that these will make him/her emerge stronger and better than he/she was before.

Eagles test before they trust; one ought to test the loyalty and commitment of peers, friends, and team members and leaders before really trusting.

Eagles prepare for training; they remove the feathers and soft grass in the nest so that the young ones get uncomfortable in preparation for flying. One need to abandon the comfort zone since there is no growth there.

Eagles find a place of renewal; as they grow old, they go through a painful process of transformation (as already discussed earlier on). Any straight thinking person should watch content that will challenge and build him/her; read books that will transform him; listen to things that are incremental to one's development so as to leave the world better than one found it.

This is why some of us devote our valuable resources like time, emotions, finance and energy to write so as to create value to the world and possibly leave it better than we found it (by God's grace). One of the definitions of success that I've come to love is "the ability to know what one doesn't need in life". This means that if I realise that I don't need to: watch this movie/programme; buy this item; listen to certain content; go to certain places; be in company with certain people; wear certain outfits; speak/talk certain words or content; then I will be successful in life. This is because, by default, if I'm able to distinguish between what I need and that I don't need, then I'll do the needful and utilize my God-given resources on only those things that create value to me and my community.

Here are the five verses that are generally included in hymnbooks and sung today.

(1) How firm a foundation, ye saints of the Lord,
Is laid for your faith in His excellent Word!
What more can He say than to you He hath said,
You, who unto Jesus for refuge have fled?

(2) Fear not, I am with thee, O be not dismayed,
For I am thy God and will still give thee aid;
I'll strengthen and help thee, and cause thee to stand
Upheld by My righteous, omnipotent hand.

(3) When through the deep waters I call thee to go,
The rivers of woe shall not thee overflow;
For I will be with thee, thy troubles to bless,
And sanctify to thee thy deepest distress.

(4) When through fiery trials thy pathways shall lie,
My grace, all sufficient, shall be thy supply;
The flame shall not hurt thee; I only design
Thy dross to consume, and thy gold to refine.

(5) The soul that on Jesus has leaned for repose,
I will not, I will not desert to its foes;
That soul, though all hell should endeavor to shake,
I'll never, no never, no never forsake.

36. O HAPPY DAY
(Nalyoka Ne Nkusenga Ggwe)
CH 310

Philip Doddridge was born in a family of nineteen brothers and sisters (good heavens, what a massive family!!). In that home, the mother Mrs. Doddridge was to have a marked influence in the life of Philip, her youngest son. She often would draw him to her knees, as they sat by the fireplace, and tell him stories from the Bible. These stories were a foundation that caused his life to be useful for the Savior. It is not known when young Philip came to know Christ as Savior, but he grew to be a mighty minister of the gospel. He became the head of an academy where he trained young men for the ministry, multiplying his influence many times over. He wrote over four hundred hymns and gospel songs.

The Doddridge family has quite a number of life lessons for us in the 21st Century to learn:

The first one is about the enormous family that was quite practical to manage during the Doddridge time but pretty uncalled for in this resource scarce and highly competitive era. It is highly questionable whether such a household would get real quality time from the parents so as guide to behavior, motivate and probably discipline. This call for being mindful of the size of family one can manage in terms of resources such as: time, emotions (love), finances, physical facilities, among others. Many a Christian families produce children in anticipation that it's the church's obligation to provide for their needs.

The second lesson is about the imperativeness of the primary/ first education experience in one's life being undertaken at home just like God model of education that was evident in the Israelite philosophy of education. In this, parents would take the primary role of instilling spiritual, mental, physical, emotional, ethical and social values in their young ones just like Mrs. Doddridge did. Thus, Proverbs 22:6 "Train up a child......" was the Hebrew idea of education where parents would build up their children's future. One day, J. F. Kennedy (former U.S President) was asked how he managed to bring up responsible children who have been so beneficial to society yet he was a very busy man. He said, "My children are my business, and my business is my children."

The third lesson is about the love to train as many young men as humanly possible for ministry is an imperative to all of us in Christian ministry as emphasized by Daniel 12:3, referring to those who brought and also trained many for ministry shall shine like stars forever. This was Philip's main inspiration in life and ministry which we equally need to religiously emulate.

This reminds of an interesting story about a boy who had a workaholic (work-craze dad) and the child was really concerned about spending some time with him. The boy (let me call him Katumba), had taken some period saving some of his pocket money so as to pay for the presence of his dad, and enjoy him for an hour without any distraction. Then, Katumba approached his dad and asked:

Katumba: Dad, how much do you earn / work for per hour?

Dad: (really moved by the question) simply hums, aahhhaammm!

Katumba: Please would you help me with some money, there is something important that I'd like to buy

Dad: (becomes impatient and infuriated by the suggestion)

Katumba: I would like to buy one hour from your busy schedule, dad, because I really miss you a lot!

(1) O happy day that fixed my choice
On Thee, my Savior and my God!
Well may this flowing heart rejoice
And tell its raptures all abroad.

Chorus:
Happy day, happy day,
When Jesus washed my sins away!
He taught me how to watch and pray
And live rejoicing every day;
Happy day, happy day,
When Jesus washed my sins away!

(2) O happy bond that seals my vows
To Him who merits all my love!
Let cheerful anthems fill His house,
While to that sacred shrine I move.

(3) It's done, the great transaction's done—
I am my Lord's and He is mine;
He drew me, and I followed on,
Thrilled to confess the voice divine.

(4) At peace, my long-divided heart,
Can in this calm assurance rest;
There is no power can make me part
From Love by which I've been possessed.

37. PEACE, BE STILL
(Mukama Gyangu Onyambe)

The author Mary Ann Baker and her only brother suffered from the same respiratory disease that had taken their parents' lives. The brother left their home in Chicago to find a warmer climate in the southern part of the United States. For a time he seemed to be improving, but then a sudden turn in his health came and he died almost immediately. Mary Ann and her sister were heartbroken. It only added to their deep grief that neither their own health nor their personal finances allowed them to claim their brother's body or to finance its return to Chicago for burial. Mary's trust in a loving God broke under the strain of her brother's death and her own diminished circumstances. "God does not care for me or mine," said Mary Ann. "This particular manifestation of what they call 'divine providence' is unworthy of a God of love." Have you ever thought the same thing? "I have always tried to believe on Christ and give the Master a consecrated life," she said, "but this is more than I can bear. What have I done to deserve this? What have I left undone that God should wreak His vengeance upon me in this way?" But as the days and the weeks went by, the God of life and love began to calm the winds and the waves of what this young woman called "her unsanctified heart." Her faith not only returned but it flourished, and she learned new things, things "too wonderful" to have known before her despair.

Gradually she came to realize that God is always a loving Heavenly Father, whether we are well or sick, rich or poor, and whether we succeed or fail, live or die.

A deeper, richer faith and more sincere trust took possession of her, and began to transform her from a rebellious daughter into an obedient and loving child.

It was at this time, in 1874, that Rev. H. R. Palmer asked her to write several songs on the Sunday school lessons for that particular year. The theme for one of the Sundays was "Christ Stilling the Tempest." As something of a personal testimonial and caring very much for the faith of others who would also be tried by personal despair, she wrote the words of the hymn that multitudes have sung for more than a century, "Master, the Tempest Is Raging."

The song is based on the story in Mark 4:36 - 41 of Jesus and his disciples caught in a fierce storm on the Sea of Galilee. But in the midst of the terror, "He arose, and rebuked the wind, and said unto the sea, Peace, be still. And the wind ceased, and there was a great calm.

The last five years have witnessed a growing number of storms, whirlwinds, earthquakes and floods country wide that are greatly linked to global warming that was occasioned by adverse human activities. From my background in Risk management (particularly Insurance), such occurrences are incidentally referred to as "Act of God" since they are above human control and management, which is quite ridiculous because we, as Christians, strongly believe that our good Lord does not cause such happenings but the adversary does. Besides, modern research has unearthed that many of these hazards, perils and risks as they are called in insurance vocabulary, are actually either ignited by human activities or practically engineered by some military agencies for reasons only known to them and used in modern military warfare. Nonetheless, while those storms have produced a great deal of damage, they have come and gone quickly. But sometimes the storms of life that we face don't end that quickly and they often leave permanent scars and damage. None of us are exempt from today's high costs of living and unemployment, from serious health problems, from family troubles, and from other woes. Nonetheless, as we face our storms of life, we ought to remember that God does care about us and He alone can give us a peace that passes understanding.

And with that in mind she began to write:

(1) Master, the tempest is raging!
The billows are tossing high!
The sky is o'ershadowed with blackness,
No shelter or help is nigh;
Carest Thou not that we perish?
How canst Thou lie asleep,
When each moment so madly is threat'ning
A grave in the angry deep?

(2) Master, with anguish of spirit
I bow in my grief today;
The depths of my sad heart are troubled;
O waken and save, I pray!
Torrents of sin and of anguish
Sweep o'er my sinking soul!
And I perish! I perish, dear Master;
O hasten, and take control!

(3) Master, the terror is over,
The elements sweetly rest;
Earth's sun in the calm lake is mirrored,
And heaven's within my breast.
Linger, O blessed Redeemer,
Leave me alone no more;
And with joy I shall make the blest harbor,
And rest on the blissful shore.

Chorus
The winds and the waves shall obey Thy will,
Peace, be still!
Whether the wrath of the storm tossed sea,
Or demons, or men, or whatever it be,
No water can swallow the ship where lies
The Master of ocean and earth and skies;
They all shall sweetly obey Thy will,
Peace, be still!
Peace, be still!
They all shall sweetly obey Thy will,
Peace, peace, be still!

38. ALL THE WAY MY SAVIOR LEADS ME
(Mu Lugendo Lwange Lwonna)
CH 259

This hymn was authored by a lady who has greatly influenced hymnody for more than one and a half century and had a troubled life just like a couple of other hymn writers. When she was just six-weeks-old, Fanny got an infection that was made worse when a phony doctor poured hot poultice on her inflamed eyes. She became almost completely blind, only able to distinguish day from night.

But just as one commentator on one television proclaimed Fanny's blindness stimulated other gifts and abilities. She had an incredible memory and was able to recite whole sections of the Bible, including the Pentateuch, the four Gospels, and all of Proverbs.

This beloved hymn came from the grateful heart of Fanny Crosby after she had received a direct answer to her prayer.

One day when she desperately needed ten dollars to pat for her rent and had no idea where she could obtain it, Fanny followed her usual custom and began to pray about the matter. A few minutes later a stranger appeared at her door with the exact amount.

"I have no way of accounting for this", she said, "except to believe that God put it into the heart of this good man to bring the money. My first thought was that it is so wonderful the way the Lord leads me, and I immediately wrote the poem".

That night, Fanny wrote the words to "All the Way My Savior Leads Me." Although the hymn was written after that specific incident, it undoubtedly represents her lifelong testimony.

While many of us might view blindness as a disability, Fanny viewed it as a gift from God and even once said that if she could meet the man who caused it, she would tell him that he innocently did her "the greatest favor in the world."

This song can be linked to the story in John 9:1-30, "And His disciples asked Him saying, 'Rabbi, who sinned, this man or his parents, that he was born blind?" Later, Christ replied that neither the man nor his parents sinned so that he became blind but it was God's will that the devil blinds him so that the saving hand (works) of God could be revealed through the man's blindness. This teaches us a great life lesson that at times our gracious Lord permits the devil to hurt our lives, just like in Job's case, so that God might manifest His redemptive power towards us His treasured and chosen children.

This hymn story teaches me a fundamental reality in life of having faith in our Eternal Lord and also to learn to be thankful in any situation. This reminds me of a popular story in a certain atheistic society whereby two men were in restaurant for lunch; one who was a Christian bowed his head to pray and thank God before he could eat. The other one was so surprised as to what on God's earth the Christian guy was doing: this prompted him to ask the Christian guy whether he was ok and what he was doing (maybe he needed help in some pain he was undergoing). The Christian man responded that he was very ok; that he was just thanking God for His providence and food, in particular. This made the atheist to laugh at him and told him that for him he uses his energy and ingenuity to earn whatever he gets through pain and he had never seen anyone (not even) God come to his rescue; that is why he doesn't need to pray or thank anyone for his fortunes and achievements in life because he deserves them. The Christian man, filled with pity, told him that he behaves like his dog, which once given food; it pounces on it without saying any thank you to its master. But in life, we ought to appreciate the fact that whatever good that comes our way, comes from our good Lord who gives blessings that are devoid of sorrow to His beloved children.

Are we that dependent on Christ to supply our needs? No matter what our supposed disability and suffering that we are currently going through, my prayer is that our good Lord makes us "blind" enough to see our need for Him on a daily basis.

> *(1) All the way my Savior leads me- What have I to ask beside?*
> *Can I doubt His tender mercy, Who*
> *through life has been my guide?*
> *Heavenly peace, divinest comfort, Here by faith in Him to dwell!*
> *For I know, whate'er befall me, Jesus doeth all things well; well.*
>
> *2) All the way my Saviour leads me; cheers*
> *each winding path I tread;*
> *Give me grace for every trial, feeds me with the living bread;*
> *Though my weary steps may falter, and my soul athirst may be,*
> *Gushing from the rock before me, lo a spring of joy I see; see.*
>
> *(3) All the way my Saviour leads me; oO the fullness of His love;*
> *Perfect rest to me is promised in my Father's house above;*
> *When I wake to life immortal, wing my fight to realms of day,*
> *This is my song through endless ages,*
> *Jesus led me all the way; way.*

39. IT IS WELL WITH MY SOUL
(Bwe Nfuna Eddembe Mu Bulamu Bwange)
CH 313

Horatio Spafford was born in North Troy, New York who became a successful lawyer and landowner in Chicago. He had a thriving legal practice, a beautiful home, a wife, four daughters and a son. He was also a devout Christian and faithful student of the Scriptures. His circle of friends included Dwight L. Moody, Ira Sankey and various other well-known Christians of the day. At the very height of his financial and professional success, Horatio and his wife Anna suffered the tragic loss of their young son due to Scarlet Fever in 1870. Shortly thereafter on October 8, 1871, the Great Chicago Fire destroyed almost every real estate investment that Spafford had.

After losing a son and his land holdings, they desired a rest. A good friend D.L. Moody invited them to join him in Europe. The plans were to enjoy a quiet time touring Europe, so they arranged to travel on the Ville Du Havre. They traveled from Chicago to New York in 1873 to start the journey, but Horatio was called back to Chicago. The family boarded the Ville Du Havre without him and set sail. He was going to join them later.

The Ville Du Havre did not make it to Europe. It was struck by a English vessel and sank quickly. "Several days later the survivors were finally landed in Cardiff, Wales and Mrs. Spafford cabled her husband 'Saved Alone'. Shortly afterwards Spafford left by ship to join his bereaved wife. While they were travelling in the area where the Ville Du Havre went down, the captain of the vessel he was on, called him up on deck. While in the area where the four daughters drowned he penned the lyrics we know today.

The Spaffords did return to Chicago and had two children. In 1881, The Spaffords left Chicago. "They left Chicago with their two young daughters and a group of friends and settled in Jerusalem. There they established the American Colony which cared for the sick and destitute. Their ministry continues today.

Philip Bliss (1838-1876), composer of many songs including Hold the Fort, Let the Lower Lights be Burning, and Jesus Loves Even Me, was so impressed with Spafford's life and the words of his hymn that he composed a beautiful piece of music to accompany the lyrics. The song was published by Bliss and Sankey, in 1876. For more than a century, the tragic story of one man has given hope to countless thousands who have lifted their voices to sing, it Is Well With My Soul. What amazes me is that Horatio Spafford's grief is not the primary focus in the song. More importantly, it was not their primary focus in life. Many people would give up after losing your assets in a fire, but they did not. I cannot imagine the pain that this family encountered with the loss of all their children

There is something special in this story. In the midst of tragedy, they continued their lives and ministry. It shows one-generation influences the next and faith prevails. Horatio only lived eight years after they moved from Chicago to Jerusalem. Bertha Spafford Vesper, one of Horatio Spafford's daughters wrote a book on the family's ministry and life called "Our Jerusalem".

I am delighted by the ministry of this family and I'd wish to assure you that there are people today who are reaching out to others through whatsApp, Facebook, Twitter and all sorts of modern communication systems through their tragedy and despite everything, they maintain, "It Is Well With My Soul".

When peace, like a river, attendeth my way,
When sorrows like sea billows roll; Whatever my lot,
Thou hast taught me to say,
It is well, it is well with my soul.

Chorus:
It is well (it is well), with my soul (with my soul),
It is well, it is well with my soul".

My sin O the joy of this glorious thought
My sin, not in part but the whole, is nailed to the cross,
And I bear it no more; praise the Lord.
Praise the Lord O my soul.

My sin, oh, the bliss of this glorious thought!
My sin, not in part but the whole,
Is nailed to the cross, and I bear it no more,
Praise the Lord, praise the Lord, O my soul!"

40. PRAISE GOD FROM WHOM ALL BLESSINGS FLOW
(Twebaza Gwe Omuva Byonna)
CH 693

Thomas Ken (1637-1711) was an Englishman and an ordained Anglican priest. He served as Rector of several parishes, was briefly chaplain to Princess Mary, and later to the British fleet. He published many poems, along with a Manual for Prayers.

He was orphaned at an early age. He then went to live with his half-sister, Anne, and her husband Izaak Walton. Thomas was enrolled by his sister into an all-boy's school, Winchester College at fourteen years, and four years later began studies at Oxford. He would return to the same school as Chaplain many years later. While there, he wrote his Manual of Prayers for the use of the Scholars of Winchester College, which he first published in 1674. It was a book of prayers for all occasions, and included (among many others) a Morning Prayer, an Evening Prayer, a prayer to use after committing a sin, a prayer for use when tempted, a prayer entitled "Acts of Shame" and another entitled "Acts of Abhorrence." In order to motivate his students in their devotions, Thomas wrote a three stanza hymn -- one verse to be sung upon waking and one before bed. The third verse was to be sung at midnight, if a boy found sleep difficult.

Today, the writing of this hymn may seem an innovative way to motivate teenage boys. In Thomas' day however, the writing of this hymn for such a purpose was somewhat revolutionary. For centuries hymns of the church were sung only by monks. Although at this point in history, Protestant churches in some countries were beginning to introduce hymns into congregational singing, it would be several years before England would officially sanction the practice (See: History of Hymns). For this reason, Thomas Ken has been called 'England's first hymnist.'

The refrain to all three verses of Thomas' hymn has since become one of the most widely-sung songs in the world, and is referred to in many circles simply as, The Doxology.

Ken Thomas, the author of this text, was a bold, outspoken 17th century Anglican bishop: his illustrious career in the ministry was stormy and colorful. He served for a time as the English chaplain at the royal court in the Hague, Holland. He was so outspoken, however, in denouncing the corrupt lives of those in authority at the Dutch capital that he was compelled to leave after a short stay.

Upon his return to England, he was appointed by King Charles 11 to be one of his chaplains. Ken continued to reveal the same spirit of boldness in rebuking the moral sins of his dissolute English monarch. Despite this, Charles always admired his courageous chaplain, calling him the good little man.

Ken established an excellent reputation at Winchester, and was eventually appointed chaplain to King Charles II. When the king decided to visit Winchester, he sent word to Ken that Nell Gwynne, the king's mistress, was to be lodged at Ken's house. Ken not only mounted loud objections, but also hired workmen to remove the roof to his house so that the king could not enforce Nell's lodgment there. In that time and place, an act of rebellion against the king could cost a person his head, but King Charles was impressed with Ken's courage. Not only did he allow Ken to live, but he even appointed him sometime later to be the Bishop of Bath and Wells.

Some years later towards the end of his life, Ken was one of seven bishops who refused to sign King James' Declaration of Indulgence. For this act of rebellion, he was arrested and imprisoned in the Tower of London by King James II, for his forward Protestant thinking — but he was later tried and acquitted. Upon his release, he quietly retired from the priesthood and went to live with some friends until his death. When he was buried at sunrise, The Doxology was sung at his funeral. He died of natural causes on March 11, 1711.

Nearly every English speaking Protestant congregation unites at least once each Saturday and Sunday in this noble overture of praise. It has been said that the Doxology has done more to teach the doctrine of the Trinity than all the theology books ever written.

The word doxology comes from two Greek words, doxa, which means glory, and logos, which means word. So a doxology is literally "a word of glory." We sing doxologies to give glory or praise to God.

There are a number of doxologies. Among the more familiar doxologies is one traditionally used in Roman Catholic worship. It begins "Glory to God in the highest, and peace to his people on earth." Another familiar doxology, The Gloria Patri, begins "Glory be to the Father, and to the Son, and to the Holy Ghost." On the contrary, this doxology in question was originally only four lines (though other stanzas have been added of recent) but these four lines might be sung more frequently than any other Christian music.

Thomas Ken's life story and courage in ministry reminds me of two great ministers in the bible who expressed such courage and resilience in their ministry: John the Baptist, who confronted Herod over charges of adultery which saw his life end by being beheaded at the request of a young girl in a bid for Herod to appease her and the mum. The second one is none other than the "embattled" prophet Jeremiah, especially in Jeremiah 8:1-13, when God sent him to declare disaster to the errant children of Israel and he had to speak the hard truth without any compromise just like any leader who is chosen by God. The lesson we ought to learn is that a godly leader doesn't take pleasure in declaring judgment but as long as it is the Lord that has sent him, he should deliver the message the way he has been instructed. On the contrary, this doesn't incite fundamentalism and confrontational approach on the part of gospel ministers to attack and continually criticize political leaders since everything must be done with wisdom and in the right proportions.

> *Praise God, from whom all blessings flow;*
> *Praise Him, all creatures here below;*
> *Praise Him above, ye heavenly host;*
> *Praise Father, Son, and Holy Ghost.*

41. I SURRENDER ALL
(Newaddeyo Gy'oli Yesu)
CH 573

Judson W. Van DeVenter (1855-1939) was raised in a Christian home. At age 17, he accepted Jesus as his Savior. He graduated at university with a degree in art and was employed successfully as a teacher and administrator of high school art. He traveled extensively, visiting the various art galleries throughout Europe.

Van DeVenter also studied and taught music. He mastered 13 different instruments, sang and composed music. He was very involved in the music ministry of his Methodist Episcopal church and eventually found himself torn between his successful teaching career and his desire to be a part of an evangelistic team. This struggle within him lasted for almost five years.

In 1896, Van DeVenter was conducting the music of a church event. It was during these meetings that he finally surrendered his desires completely to God -- He made the decision to become a full-time evangelist. As he submitted completely to the will of his Lord, a song was born in his heart.

"I Surrender All" was put to music by Winfield S. Weeden (1847-1908), who published this and many other hymns in several volumes. Weeden so loved this song that the words "I Surrender All" were put on his tombstone.

The song is premised on Jesus' strong caution as recorded by Luke, in Luke 14:33, "Any of you who does not give up everything cannot be My disciple". Besides, this was further expounded by Paul's epistle to the Philippians on the topic of the priceless value of knowing Christ in Philippians 3:7-8, "I once thought these things were valuable, but now I consider them worthless because of what Christ has done. Yes, everything else is worthless when compared with the infinite value of knowing Christ Jesus my Lord. For His sake, I have discarded everything else, counting it all as garbage, so that I could gain Christ."

When Paul spoke of "these things", he was referring to his credentials, credits, and successes. After showing that he could beat the Judaizers at their own game (being proud of who they were and what they had done), Paul showed that it was the wrong game. Be careful of considering past achievements so important that they get in the way of your relationship with Christ. After Paul considering all his life achievements "worthless" when compared to the greatness of knowing Christ, he emphasized that the ultimate goal of every Christian and of everything in life should be the knowledge of Christ Jesus. Paul gave up everything: family, friendship, prestige of his professorship and being a Pharisee, and freedom; in order to know Christ and His resurrection power. We, too, have access to this knowledge and this power, but we may have to make sacrifices to enjoy it fully as did both Paul and DeVenter during their lives.

To surrender all means self-denial or carrying one's cross and follow Jesus. We live in a "we-generation" or "I-generation", where everything is about I/we that is indicative of selfishness; but carrying the cross means self-denial for the sake of others and surrendering all to Christ.

This reminds me of a story of a man who felt like his cross (troubles, temptations and trials) were to heavy and much heavier than anyone else's. After pleading to God to help him at least exchange with another one, he was sent to the "Crosses" room (where crosses- each one's burdens are stored) so as get a lighter cross that he would feel ok with. After quite a long period of searching for the best cross, he ended up unconsciously picking his cross again as the lightest cross amongst the many crosses in the room. Implying that though unhappy, his cross was way lighter than any other person's troubles, trial and hardships.

All to Jesus, I surrender;
All to Him I freely give;
I will ever love and trust Him,
In His presence daily live.

Refrain:
I surrender all, I surrender all,
All to Thee, my bless'd Savior,
I surrender all.

All to Jesus, I surrender;
Lord, I give myself to Thee;
Fill me with Thy love and power;
Let Thy blessing fall on me.

All to Jesus I surrender;
Humbly at His feet I bow,
Worldly pleasures all forsaken;
Take me, Jesus, take me now.

All to Jesus, I surrender;
Make me, Savior, wholly Thine;
Let me feel the Holy Spirit,
Truly know that Thou art mine.

All to Jesus I surrender;
Now I feel the sacred flame.
O the joy of full salvation!
Glory glory to His name

42. NEARER MY GOD TO THEE
(Katonda Onsembeze)
A & M 352   CH 382

Sarah Flower Adams wrote the words and her sister, Eliza Flower, wrote the music. Together they wrote a number of hymns, but this is the only one still in common use today. Sarah (the author of the words) enjoyed a successful career on the stage playing Lady MacBeth in Shakespearean drama, but retired from the stage due to health problems. Sarah (1805-1848) was a British actress, dramatic poet and Unitarian hymn writer. After Adams' performance in London's 1837 MacBeth, she received rave reviews. Her desire was to continue with the theatre indefinitely, but frail health interrupted her plans. And so she took to writing poems and hymns. A pastor from the Unitarian church was visiting with Adams' family one afternoon. He mentioned that he was having difficulty finding a hymn that represented his following week's sermon, taken from Genesis 28:11-19 (The story of Jacob's dream). Sarah volunteered to write a hymn for the occasion. Within the week, "Nearer My God to Thee" was born. Not long thereafter, her sister, Eliza, came down with tuberculosis. Sarah, determined to nurse her, came down with the disease as well, and both died at a relatively young age.

The beautiful hymn has touched many lives, and has even found its way into the modern theatre that Adams so dearly loved. The song has been sung and/or played in several TV and Hollywood films, including the Academy Award-winning films San Francisco (1936), and Titanic (1953, 1958, 1997). One true life Canadian survivor of the 1912 RMS Titanic tragedy reported that the band did indeed play "Nearer My God to Thee" as the ship was sinking.

The song can be linked to King David's counsel to humanity in Psalms 73:28, "But it is good for me to draw near to God; I have put my trust in the Lord God, that I may declare all Your works."

The message of the hymn is that every experience, good or bad, can draw us nearer to God, who gives us comfort and strength.

- Bearing a cross brings us nearer to God.
- Darkness brings us nearer to God.
- Angels bring us nearer to God.
- And grief brings us nearer to God.

The things that the hymn mentions (a cross, darkness, grief) tend to be difficulties. Sometimes when life is good we tend to forget that we need God. It is the difficult times that reinforce our deep need for God's grace — that do, indeed, bring us nearer to God.

Many folks associate this hymn with events related to death or extreme suffering but that would be getting the whole point wrong since it is not only during such situations in life that we need to be nearer our God. He would love to see us very close to Him during prosperity, success, happiness so as to guide us in making rational decisions of our daily living during such happy moments since research and experience have proved that normally it is amidst such joyful moments that human beings actually make irrational and foolish life decisions that destroy their dear lives. Therefore, Adams' composition emphasized our reliance on God during sorrowful as well as cheerful circumstances in our life because the fact is that we ought not to walk alone in a world whose ruler is the devil as Christ highlighted it in the scriptures. How I pray that we all take this hymn as an encouragement to always seek God's face and nearness as we tread this life's troubled path!

> *Nearer my God to Thee, nearer to Thee!*
> *Even though it be a cross that raises me!*
> *Still all my song shall be, nearer my God to Thee,*
> *Nearer my God to Thee, nearer to Thee.*
>
> *Though like a wanderer, daylight all gone,*
> *Darkness be over me, my rest a stone;*
> *Yet in my dreams I'd be nearer my God to Thee,*
> *Nearer my God to Thee, nearer to Thee.*

43. WERE YOU THERE ?
SDAH 158

This is an African-American spiritual whose author is known only to God. These spirituals were popular among African slaves quite early around the beginning of the 19th Century. They started becoming known in the wider church (white congregations) after the Civil War, which ended in 1865. Those who were oppressed by slavery would sing together for encouragement. Believers would reflect on Christ's sufferings and the consolation of the gospel.

The Fisk Jubilee Singers, African-American students from Fisk University, made a major contribution to the awareness of this spiritual when they went on a tour in 1871 to raise money. They performed to acclaim in the United States, England, and Europe, and made $150,000 to support their college.

Envision the heart-felt singing of this hymn before the civil war. The All Music Guide recalls, "The song opens in the traditional 'lining out' style of American country congregations in which the preacher or choir leader sings the first line and the choir or congregation responds. Thus, the (usually) solo voice sings 'Were you there when they crucified my Lord?'... Then the chorus responds in full harmony echoing the same words..."

The memory of Calvary's events follow in each stanza:

    (2) Were you there when they nailed Him to the tree?

    (3) Were you there when they pierced Him in the side?

    (4) Were you there when the sun refused to shine?

    (5) Were you there when they laid Him in the tomb?

    (6) Were you there when they rolled the stone away?

    (7) Did you know He is risen from the dead? (repeat)

This song has captured the hearts of people for at least a century and a half. One reason is that it speaks clearly of the death and resurrection of our Lord—the central events of our faith. We often sing it (or hear it sung) whenever the preacher is preaching from a crucifixion or resurrection text—but it is always appropriate to bring the death and resurrection of Jesus to the forefront of the worshiping community.

This is one of the hymns that explicitly depict Christ's passion basing on the New Testament narratives of Matthew 27:31-56; 28:1-15. The first stanza asks:

"Were you there when they crucified my Lord? Were you there when they crucified my Lord? Oh! Sometimes it causes me to tremble, tremble, tremble. Were you there when they crucified my Lord?" From my childhood, I've watched films representing the life and ministry of Jesus Christ but, one called the " The Passion of the Christ" stands out from them. This is because, just like, the hymn "Were you there?", gives a lot more glimpses on the suffering of my Lord than any other actors I've watched, and even if one could be a hard-core criminal, one can't escape shedding tears before such horrible devices and acts of a fallen humanity. The first lines pose the rhetorical question, "Were you there?" The assumed answer was "no," but the song takes the singer back by envisioning those redemptive events by faith.

But as in the Pauline writings in Romans 5:12: "Therefore, just as through one man sin entered the world, and death through sin, and thus death spread to all men, because all sinned.", the answer to the rhetorical question turns out to be "Yes, I was there." This is because according to Genesis 3:1-24, everyone was in Adam at the dawn of history, though our personal life began in the recent past; we were all in Adam's position; since Adam was constituted by God to represent all of the human race. Verses 15-19 bring the gist of this mystery and doctrine explicitly: "... by the one man's offense [Adam's] many died... For the judgment which came from one offense resulted in condemnation ... by the one man's offense, death reigned through the one... through one man's offense, judgment came to all men, resulting in condemnation... by one man's disobedience many were made sinners..."

A major reason for this song's popularity is the simplicity of the words. It repeats "Were you there?" over and over again.

Were you there when they crucified my Lord?

Were you there when they nailed him to a tree?

Were you there when they laid him in a tomb?

Were you there when he rose up from the dead?

The phrases are short, and the words are common and easy to understand. These are words used in the daily life, though in this song they take on the character of atonement. It is meant to be sung slowly, thoughtfully, and even mournfully; because it speaks of the Lord's suffering and death. However, the mood changes sharply in the last verse—the one that speaks of resurrection.

> 1) *Were you there when they crucified my Lord?*
> *Were you there when they crucified my Lord?*
> *Oh! Sometimes it causes me to tremble, tremble, tremble.*
> *Were you there when they crucified my Lord?*
>
> *Were you there when he rose up from the dead?*
> *Were you there when he rose up from the dead?*
> *Oh! Sometimes I feel like shouting glory, glory, glory!*
> *Were you there when he rose up from the dead?*

44. MORE ABOUT JESUS
(Ntegeza Ebya Yesu)
CH 525

Eliza Edmunds Hewitt was born in 1851, graduated as valedictorian of her normal school class and went on to teach in the public schools in Philadelphia. All of this suddenly ended when she suffered an incapacitating back injury and became bed-ridden for an extended period of time. From a human perspective, no one could blame her for having been bitter with God for her illness, and possibly having complained to God about the unfairness of all that is happening to as many folks have and always do in their lives. On the contrary, she never ever complained except taking more time to learn about Jesus. And on her bed, she studied English literature and began to sing and write. She took this time to learn more about Jesus. This was her prayer to her Lord, that He opens her eyes so she would see more of Him and reflects more of Him.

More about Jesus let me learn,

More of His holy will discern; Spirit of God, my teacher be, Showing the things of Christ to me.

Some of her poems became known to Professor John R. Sweeney, who set them to music. Eliza's back condition improved and she was able to resume some of her duties, though she struggled with pain the rest of her life. She became Sunday school superintendent of the Northern Home for Friendless Children and later at Calvin Presbyterian Church. She died in 1920.

This hymn can be likened to Apostle Peter's counsels in 1 Peter 2:7, "Therefore, to you who believe, He is precious; but to those who are disobedient, 'the stone which the builders rejected has become the chief cornerstone." Besides, Isaiah 40:31, "But those who wait on the Lord shall renew their strength; they shall mount up with wings like eagles, they shall run and not be weary, they shall walk and not faint."

Many times, we fail to view life events in the right perspective as our God would expect us but confine ourselves to the small perspective/ picture that makes us lose the point right away. If it wasn't Eliza's sickness and extended period of being bed-ridden, she possibly wouldn't have identified and later developed her talents in literature and poetry that led to such beautiful and spiritually edifying poem-turned-music text. Unless we crave to learn how God really operates, and that He does everything for our own good but in His assigned time, we shall live a life of complaining, anguish, desperation and devoid of real meaning. Fortunately, some folks were blessed to learn and appreciate this reality, and such were hymn writers as: Spafford, Crosby, Watts, Flint, Baxter; and now Eliza Hewitt who made good use of their situations to learn more about Jesus, to allow Him live out in their lives, but also bless other people through the tragic and troublesome lives they led. This is my humble prayer that henceforth, may we purpose to learn about Jesus so that we can also share that knowledge with others who are desperately looking for happiness, satisfaction and fulfilment in this world which can only give them sorrows and uncertainty.

This narrative reminds me of a story of an old poor man, so poor that he'd never slept in a house nor worn shoes in life. Some Christian youths in a certain township were moved by compassion regarding his desperate life that they built him a house and taught him how to have a decent life. Unfortunately, it was the time of El Nino (stormy rains) in Kenya, so his house was all washed away with him to a river as he had slept soundly one night. Early in the morning, he said, "Why only me, God?", until he went back to where his house was, and in anguish and despair, he started touching the ground. He realized something glittering, which later turned out to be gold; so he went without informing these youths, who had actually forsaken him ever since the incident and talked to some white man (Muzungu) who agreed to buy the land off. He became so rich that instead of banking his money, he bought a bank in Poland, and later a city was named after him. It is said that this man actually bailed out the Polish economy during the historical 1930s World Economic Recession, (which as economists, we believe is the mother of all global economic crises that have ever happened since then), when the Polish economy was in shambles. Just like Eliza's back injury, these floods brought a new life to this old once poor man that even now, records hold him in high esteem globally.

> *More about Jesus I would know, more*
> *of His grace to others show;*
> *More of His saving fullness see, more*
> *of His love who died for me.*
>
> *Chorus*
> *More, more about Jesus, more about Jesus;*
> *More of His saving fullness see, more*
> *of His love who died for me.*
>
> *More about Jesus let me learn, more of His holy will discern;*
> *Spirit of God, my teacher be, showing the things of Christ to me.*
>
> *More about Jesus; on His throne, riches in glory all His own;*
> *More of His kingdom's sure increase; more*
> *of His coming Prince of Peace.*

45. 'TIS SO SWEET TO TRUST IN JESUS
(Tukwesiga Omulokozi)
CH 588

Louisa M. R. Stead (1850-1917), had planned a family outing with her husband and four-year-old daughter Lily at the beach on Long Island Sound, New York. As the family was enjoying their picnic lunch they heard, coming from the sound, desperate cries for help. They spotted a young boy drowning in the sea. Mr. Stead rushed to rescue the boy, but, as often happens; the struggling and terrified child pulled his rescuer under the water with him. Both drowned as his horrified wife and daughter watched helplessly. Louisa and Lily were left to experience poverty, loneliness and deprivation in their life.

Louisa Stead struggled with the question of why her husband, who with her was committed to serving Christ, should lose his life in such a tragedy, leaving her and her daughter in desperation and all of the promise of his life lost. In the midst of such anxiety, one day she found food and money dropped/ left for her on the doorstep. She was so defeated in her thoughts, after having spent quite some good time complaining and almost cursing God for all her life circumstances. In the tragic drowning of her husband, a young wife and mother affirmed through her tears that there is comfort and grace in Christ. She surrendered her doubts and despairs and, in this dark hour of her life, composed the words that have been a comfort to many in times of stress and loss in 1882. Later, Louisa and Lily left for South Africa to serve as missionaries for twenty five years in both South Africa and Southern Rhodesia, and where she found a new husband, and they led a missionary life thereafter. Her Missionary comrads in Southern Rhodesia wrote this tribute after her death: "Her influence goes on as our five thousand native Christians continually sing her hymn in their native language."

This reminds me of a powerful scripture in 2 Cor. 5:7, "For we walk but faith, not by sight." And also in Jeremiah 29:11-12, "For I know the thoughts I think toward you, says the Lord, thoughts of peace and not of evil, to give you a future and a hope. Then you will call upon Me and go and pray to Me, and I will listen to you."

We too may be called upon to enter the miserable deserts of barrenness, poverty, deprivation, destitution, marriage break-ups, and failure to get a spouse, joblessness, loneliness, shame or the dark valley of anguish. In such times we can also know the peace that comes through trust in Jesus and go on to fruitful service for Him. It is only the steadfast trust in our Eternal Savior that you will become triumphant. May we in our sunlit days, as well as in our darkest hours, know the sweetness, the serenity, and the strength that comes when we trust in Jesus.

This hymn also reminds me of the miraculous interventions that our God has been demonstrating to His own from the Old Testament times to the contemporary post-modern generation in the way of break-through in spiritual battles, employment, marriage, studies, leadership, and a host of many others. We are all living testimonies of what our Loving God has done in our lives. Unfortunately, the devil often robs us of the opportunity to remember all God's triumph in our life so as to praise His victorious name or the opportunity to count on Him in the face of such threatening circumstances. Hence, the precious hymn of the church had its origin in the crucible of a tragic loss that was borne by Louisa Stead of which we are thankful that God helped her to grow in faith and also share such experiences with us that have witnessed the end of the times.

(1) 'Tis so sweet to trust in Jesus,
And to take Him at His Word;
Just to rest upon His promise,
And to know, "Thus says the Lord!"

Refrain
Jesus, Jesus, how I trust Him!
How I've proved Him o'er and o'er
Jesus, Jesus, precious Jesus!
O for grace to trust Him more!

(2) O how sweet to trust in Jesus,
Just to trust His cleansing blood;
And in simple faith to plunge me
'Neath the healing, cleansing flood!

(3) Yes, 'tis sweet to trust in Jesus,
Just from sin and self to cease;
Just from Jesus simply taking
Life and rest, and joy and peace.

(4) I'm so glad I learned to trust Thee,
Precious Jesus, Savior, Friend;
And I know that Thou art with me,
Wilt be with me to the end.

46. I MUST TELL JESUS
SDAH 485

Elisha A. Hoffman (1839-1929) loved the Lord and chose to show it by working to help people who others call, "down and out". One day, he was visiting a woman who was in great pain, so discouraged, sorrowful and afflicted in through her life. She relieved her heavy heart, concluding with the question, "Brother Hoffman, what shall I do?" Hoffman gave her great counsels that, "You cannot do better than to take all of your sorrows to Jesus. You must tell Jesus." For a moment, she seemed lost in meditation as if she'd either not understood what she'd just been told or despising the counsels she'd just received. Then her eyes lighted as she exclaimed, "Yes, I must tell Jesus". As Hoffman left her home, and later had a vision of that joy-illuminated face. He heard all along his pathway the echo, "I must tell Jesus. I must tell Jesus" and these words rang in his ears without going away. He wrote promptly the song after reaching home in which he expressed that not only do we need to go to Jesus but also to tell Him about our worldly temptations that attract us each day.

This hymn story rhymes so well with the Apostle Peter's epistle: 1 Peter 5:6-7, "Therefore, humble yourselves under the mighty hand of God, that He may exalt you in due time, casting all your care (anxiety) upon Him, for He cares for you." A certain translation of my local language Luganda portrays it quite good, where there is, "He cares for you", the version uses (loosely translated) "He puts my anxiety on His heart" which indicates the highest level of care, concern confidentiality and thoughtfulness on the part of our loving Lord.

We live in a world with the highest levels of moral decay, and virtues like confidentiality and thoughtfulness only remained in the dictionary as vocabulary but hardly, if ever, are practiced in the real world which ironically has better systems of ethics in various professions such as medical, investment management, law, accountancy, counseling, and among other. For example, in my profession of investment management, the biggest part of our study/ training in CFA (Chartered Financial Analyst) is premised on ethics but normally in the real investment world many other realities overshadow that important virtue.

From a Christian perspective, I find it sickening and not so appropriate for fellow Christians to always tell their challenges to people because in most cases, that information will leak to some others who were not intended to consume it. This reminds me of a common saying among the Batoro (a certain tribe in Western Uganda), "Okigambire nyowe okizikire" loosely translated as "Now that you have told me this story, you have almost buried it- no one will ever get to know it after." On the contrary, it is said that whoever tells you that, has someone in whom he/ she confides secrets, so he/ she will also tell that person who will also do the same, and at the end it will become an open secret or common knowledge. This gives me more reason, as a church Elder, always to recommend Christians to *tell Jesus* about their troubles/ anxiety because it is only Him who can keep it on His heart. My basic counsel here is that, though personally, I can't go on splashing people's details (anxiety), I'd love to see them establish an intimate relationship and constant communication with their heavenly Father for any detail of their life other than telling people who actually in most cases will ridicule them and not keep it on their hearts.

I must tell Jesus all of my trials;
I cannot bear these burdens alone;
In my distress He kindly will help me;
He ever loves and cares for His own.
Chorus
I must tell Jesus! I must tell Jesus!
I cannot bear my burdens alone;
I must tell Jesus! I must tell Jesus!
Jesus can help me, Jesus alone.

I must tell Jesus all of my troubles;
He is a kind, compassionate friend;
If I but ask Him, He will deliver,
Make of my troubles quickly an end.

Tempted and tried, I need a great Savior;
One who can help my burdens to bear;
I must tell Jesus, I must tell Jesus;
He all my cares and sorrows will share.

O how the world to evil allures me!
O how my heart is tempted to sin!
I must tell Jesus, and He will help me
Over the world the victory to win.

47. ROCK OF AGES, CLEFT FOR ME
(Olwazi Lw'edda N'edda Ggwe)
A & M 210   CH 474

Augustus Montague Toplady (1740 - 1778) was an unusual child. His father died when he was very young and so he was raised by his mother who adored and spoiled him. He was not very well liked by his peers or his relatives, partly because they did not relate to his extreme intelligence, and partly because he was sickly and fearful.

Controversy followed Toplady throughout his short 38 years of life, but he did not let that stop him. At a very young age he showed a keen interest in developing a relationship with God. By age 12 he was preaching sermons, and at age 14 he began writing hymns. He was ordained as an Anglican priest at the age of 22. Although some thought him to be arrogant and obstinate, excerpts from his writings verify that he was a devoted and humble follower of Christ.

An example of one of the many poems Toplady wrote between the ages of 15 and 16 years:

Refining Fuller, make me clean,

On me thy costly pearl bestow:

Thou art thyself the pearl I prize,

The only joy I seek below.

An excerpt from his personal journal, at age 27:

O, my Lord let not my ministry be approved only, or tend to be no more than conciliating the esteem and affections of my people to thy unworthy messenger; but to do the work of thy grace upon their hearts: call in thy chosen; seal and edify thy regenerate; and command thy everlasting blessing upon their souls! Save me from self-opinion, and from self-seeking; and may they cease from man, and look solely upon thee.

As we've just evidenced from his intelligence and background, Reverend Toplady a was circuit-riding preacher (he was a preacher/ church minister but during his free time, he was a circuit-rider of horses also as a career). It is believed that one day, as he was on the circuit-riding part of his life on his horse, the heavens suddenly opened and there commenced a terrific storm of heavy thunder and lightning . Rather frightened, he slid off his saddle; he found refuge and safety in the crack of a large rock nearby. While there, he took time to ponder all his life and how it was almost ended by a lightning; he contemplated over the rock that had saved his life. This took his mind back to the early church in the desert whereby Christ acted as the Rock that shielded the Hebrews (Israelites) from all adversities and adversaries such as: the hostile tribes; hunger; thirst; scorching sunshine; among others during their way to the Promised Land. He later made meaning of King David's Psalms like in Psalms 18:1-6, about God being our Eternal Rock; that experience led Augustus Toplady to write the hymn, "Rock of ages, cleft for me let me hide myself in Thee."

As already highlighted, there are lots of parallels between the hymn and Psalms 18:1-6, "................The Lord is my Rock and my Fortress and my Deliverer; my God, my strength, in whom I will trust; my Shield and the horn of my salvation, my stronghold............"

Psalms 18:1-6 is a direct duplicate of 2 Samuel 22:1-, and it is believed to have been written toward the end of David's life when there was peace. God is praised for His glorious works and blessings through the years. God's protection of His people is limitless and can take many forms. David characterized God's care with four (4) military symbols, God is like:

> A Rock; that can't be moved by any who would harm us.
> A Fortress/ place of safety; where the enemy can't follow us. A place of safety- high above our enemy. So, if you need protection, look to God.
>
> A Shield; that comes between us and the enemy (harm).
>
> A Power; that saves, a symbol of might that can save us.

Rock of ages, cleft for me
let me hide myself in thee;
let the water and the blood,
from thy wounded side which flowed,
be of sin the double cure;
save from wrath and make me pure.

Not the labors of my hands
can fulfill thy law's commands;
could my zeal no respite know,
could my tears forever flow,
all for sin could not atone;
thou must save, and thou alone.

Nothing in my hand I bring,
simply to the cross I cling;
naked, come to thee for dress;
helpless, look to thee for grace;
foul, I to the fountain fly;
wash me, Savior, or I die.

While I draw this fleeting breath,
when mine eyes shall close in death,
when I soar to worlds unknown,
see thee on thy judgment throne,
Rock of Ages, cleft for me,
let me hide myself in thee.

48. WHAT A FRIEND WE HAVE IN JESUS
(Tulina Omukwano Gwaffe)
CH 588

Joseph Scriven was a man acquainted with grief; born in County Down, Ireland. He aspired as a young man to follow in his father's footsteps as a Royal Marine, but his poor health made that impossible. Then he fell in love and was engaged to be married in 1840, but his fiancée drowned before their wedding could take place.

To put as much distance as possible between himself and that tragedy, Scriven then moved to Canada. While living there, he became engaged again with another lady, but his fiancée became ill and also died before they could be married. In his grief, Scriven determined never to be again in the craze of marriage, and to devote himself to a life of service. He was especially known for carrying a bucksaw and cutting firewood for people in need.

Scriven received word that his widowed mother, Jane Medlicott Scriven of Ireland (70 years at the time) was going through a particular sorrowful time of illness in Dublin. Due to financial constraints, he couldn't afford to return to Ireland, so he sent his mother a poem in the hope that it would comfort her. The poem written in 1857 began, "What a friend we have in Jesus, all our sins and grief to bear! What a privilege to carry everything to God in prayer!" Initially, He never intended anyone would see it, but a friend saw it scribbled on scratch paper while nursing him when he was ill, and it was published soon afterwards, titled, "Pray without Ceasing." He later submitted a copy of his poem to a religious journal, where it was published. A few years later, in 1866, he died.

In 1875, Ira Sankey had just returned from England and was working with Philip Bliss on a new song book called, Gospel Hymns, No. 1. After the completed work was delivered to the publisher, Mr. Sankey picked up a small pamphlet of Sunday school hymns that had been published in Richmond, Virginia. Since Charles Converse was a good friend, Mr. Sankey took one of his tunes and put the words with it and named it: "What A Friend We Have in Jesus." It was the last hymn to be added to the book, but it became the first as a favorite. This hymn has always been one of the best-known hymns in America. Missionaries took it abroad, where people sang it in many languages. This hymn has maintained its popularity for a century and a half basically because the man acquainted with both grief and living faith helps us to see that faith can triumph over grief.

To change the focus of the song off of Prayer, the last verse was omitted:

> *Blessed Saviour, Thou hast promised*
> *Thou wilt all our burdens bear*
> *May we ever, Lord, be bringing all to Thee in earnest prayer.*
> *Soon in glory bright unclouded there will be no need for prayer,*
> *Rapture, praise and endless worship will*
> *be our sweet portion there.*

Christ talking about friends, this is what he has to say in John 15:13-15, "Greater love has no one than this, than to lay down one's life for his friends. You are My friends if you do whatever I command you. No longer do I call you servants, for a servant doesn't know what his master is doing; but I have called you friends, for all things that I heard from My Father I have made known to you."

Like Scriven, we too may be called upon to enter the miserable wilderness of barrenness, desolation, poverty, deprivation, destitution, marriage break-ups, and failure to get a spouse, joblessness, loneliness, shame or the dark valley of anguish. In such times we can also know the peace that comes through having a friend in Jesus and go on to fruitful service for Him. It is only the steadfast friendship with our Eternal Savior that you can become triumphant. May we in our bright days, as well as in our gloomy hours, know the sweetness, the serenity, and the strength that comes when we have a friend in Jesus.

We are all living testimonies of what our Loving God has done in our lives. Unfortunately, the devil often robs us of the opportunity to remember all God's triumphs in our life so as to praise His victorious name or the opportunity to count on Him in the face of such threatening circumstances. Hence, the precious and popular hymn of the church had its origin in the crucible of a tragic loss that was borne by John Scriven of which we are thankful that God helped him to grow in faith and also share such experiences with us the post-modern lukewarm Christians.

What a friend we have in Jesus, all our sins and grief to bear;
What a privilege to carry everything to God in prayer!
O what a peace we often forfeit, O what needless pain we bear,
All because we do not carry everything to God in prayer.

Have we trials and temptations? Is there trouble anywhere?
We should never be discouraged; take it to Lord in prayer!
Can we find a friend so faithful, who will all our sorrows share?
Jesus knows our every weakness; take it to the Lord in prayer!

Are we weak and heavy laden, cumbered with a load of care?
Precious Saviour, still our refuge, take it to the Lord in prayer!
Do your friends despise, forsake thee?
Take it to the Lord in prayer!
In His arms He'll take and shield thee,
thou will find a solace there.

49. HE LIVES, (I Serve A Risen Saviour)
SDAH 251

Alfred H. Ackley was born on January 21, 1887. His father, a Methodist preacher and musically gifted man, gave Alfred his foundation in music at an early age. Alfred went on to study harmony and composition in New York and at the Royal Academy of Music in London. He played the piano and cello and showed great promise as a composer. After his training in music, Ackley went on to graduate from Westminster Theological Seminary in Maryland, and was ordained as a Presbyterian minister. He served as pastor in several states of the United States, and worked for a few years with evangelist Billy Sunday and the Rodeheaver Music Company. Ackley's musical endeavors were so appreciated that he was awarded an honorary Doctor of Sacred Music degree by John Brown University in Arkansas. Over time, he felt a call to preach and pastored for many years, but never stopped writing music and hymns

Alfred Ackley often worked in collaboration with, and is often confused with, his brother Bentley Ackley (1872-1958), who was also a talented musician, worked for the Rodeheaver Music Company, and who travelled with the Billy Sunday team for eight years as a secretary/pianist. Bentley Ackley played the melodeon, piano, organ, coronet, clarinet and piccolo.

Alfred Ackley wrote lyrics and/or music for more than 1,500 religious and secular songs, including lyrics for the still well loved "I Never Walk Alone", and "He Lives!"

One particular morning, Easter Sunday in 1932, Rev. Ackley was preparing for his services of the day. As he was shaving, he tuned in to the radio in time to hear a special Easter broadcast.

"Good morning!" The well-known liberal preacher began.

"It's Easter! You know folks, it really doesn't make any difference to me if Christ be risen or not. As far as I am concerned, His body could be as dust in some Palestinian tomb. The main thing is, His truth goes marching on!"

Rev. Ackley was furious. "It's a lie!" he shouted at the radio set, forgetting that the speaker could not hear him. Mrs. Ackley did hear him, however, and questioned, "Why are you shouting so early in the morning?"

"Didn't you hear what that good-for-nothing preacher said?" he replied. "He said it didn't matter whether Christ be risen or not!"

Rev. Ackley knew that the truth of the resurrection DID matter, as evidenced by a conversation he had had with a young Jewish man just a few weeks prior. Prior to the Easter Sunday incident, he had been preaching during an evangelistic crusade, and after one service, a young man doubting Christ's resurrection had asked him, "Why should I worship a dead Jew?" Rev. Ackley had replied in trying to persuade the young man so that he can give his heart to Christ, he stated, "He lives! That's the whole point. He isn't dead; He's alive!" Ackley added, "He lives here and now! Jesus is more alive today than ever before. I can prove it by my own experience, and as well as the testimonies of countless thousands of people." Later that evening the young man gave his heart to Christ.

Rev. Ackley, in telling the story later, said that he preached that Easter Sunday quite differently than he had ever preached before, but at the end of the day, still felt that he had not yet said everything he wanted to say!

His wife sized up the situation and said, "Listen here, Alfred

Ackley, it's time you did that which you can do best. Why don't you write a song about it and then maybe you'll feel better. You'll have something that will go on telling the story." That very night, Rev. Alfred Ackley wrote out the words, and then composed the melody just as it appears in our hymnals today.

This hymn links directly to Paul's words to the Christians in Rome and its vast empire, in Romans 14:9, "For to this end, Christ died and rose again, that He might be Lord of both the dead and the living." That is why we, as Christians proudly join Ackley in the affirmation that, we serve a risen Saviour who is in the world today; we know that He is living, whatever men (atheists, existentialists, naturalists, and other philosophical schools of thought that don't believe in Christ's living) may say; we see His hand of mercy, we hear His voice of cheer; and just the time we need Him, He is always near. Above all, when they ask us how we know He lives, the answer is, "He lives within our hearts."

I serve a risen Saviour, He's in the world today;
I know that He is living, whatever men may say;
I see His hand of mercy, I hear His voice of cheer,
And just the time I need Him, He's always near.

Chorus
He lives, he lives Christ Jesus lives today!
He walks with me and talks with me along life's narrow way.
He lives, He lives, salvation to impart!
You ask me how I know He lives? He lives within my heart!

Rejoice, rejoice, O Christian, lift up your voice
And sing Eternal hallelujahs to Jesus Christ the King!
The hope of all who seek Him, the help of all who find,
None other is so loving, so good and kind.

50. I GAVE MY LIFE FOR THEE
(Nawaayo Obulamu)
CH 230

Frances Ridley Havergal wrote one of her most famous poems while she was in Dusseldorf, Germany. She had gone to Germany to do some specialized study, and there she was staying in the house of a pastor. While there, she saw a copy of Sternburg's great painting: "The CRUCIFIXION" which had a picture of the crucified Savior. It was January 10, 1858. She had come in tired, and sitting down before the picture the Savior's eyes seemed to rest upon her The title above the picture was, "All this I did for thee; what has thou done for Me?" She read the words, and the lines of her hymn flashed upon her. She wrote them in pencil on a scrap of paper but looking them over, she thought them so poor that she tossed them into the stove/ fire but a light wind blew the paper out of the fire and onto the fireside. Feeling that this might have been fortunate, Miss Havergal took the slightly-scorched paper, folded it, and sent it to her father in England.

He composed a tune to match the words and had it published. However, the tune we now use with this superb poem was written years later by P. P. Bliss, an associate of D. L. Moody.

This particular hymn asks some extremely touching questions of each of us and this is proved by the author's repetition of those questions in each of the verses. These rhetorical questions are much more significant to us today as they were in the 1860's when they were written. There are four key questions the author uses to determine our commitment to Christ. One of the great things about these questions is that we can find examples of how to or how not to answer them in Scripture.

> *I gave, I gave My life for thee, what hast thou given for Me?*
> *I left, I left it all for thee, hast thou left aught for Me?*
>
> *I've borne, I've borne it all for thee, what hast thou borne for Me?*

I bring, I bring rich gifts to thee, what hast thou brought to Me?

Great gifts I brought to thee: What hast thou brought to Me?

These pointing questions can only be answered by Paul's plea to the Christian church in Rome, Romans 12:1-2, "I beseech you therefore, brethren, by the mercies of God, that you present your bodies a living sacrifice, holy, acceptable to God, which is your reasonable service. And do not be conformed to this world, but be transformed by the renewing of your mind, that you may prove what is that good and acceptable and perfect will of God."

God wants us to offer ourselves, not animals, as living sacrifices by daily laying aside our own desires to follow Him, putting all our energy and resources at His disposal and trusting Him to guide us. We do this out of gratitude that our sins have been forgiven. He has good , pleasing, and perfect plans for His children. He wants us to be transformed people with renewed minds, living to honour and obey Him. For this, we have a reason to joyfully give ourselves as living sacrifices for His service.

This is one of the hymns that explicitly depicts Christ's passion basing on the New Testament narratives of Matthew 27:31-56; 28;1-15. The first stanza asks:

" I gave My life for thee, My precious blood I shed, that thou might ransomed be, and raised up from the dead; I gave, I gave My life for thee, what hast thou given for Me? I gave, I gave My life for thee, what hast thou given for Me?" From my childhood, I've watched films representing the life and ministry of Jesus Christ but, one called the "The Passion of the Christ" stands out from them. This is because, just like, the hymn question "I've borne, I've borne it all for thee, what hast thou borne for Me?", gives a lot more glimpses on suffering of my Lord than any other actors I've watched, and even if one could be a hard-core criminal, one can't help shading tears before such horrible devices and acts of a fallen humanity. The fourth lines pose the rhetorical question, "I left, I left it all for thee, hast thou left aught for Me?" As highlighted above, the only satisfactory response to those challenging questions is the dedication of one's life to be obedient and a servant of the will of God all through our mortal life since there is nothing we can give back to Christ in exchange of His sacrifice nor is there any sufferings we can bear that can be equivalent to what He bore for our sins.

> *I gave My life for thee, My precious blood I shed,*
> *That thou might ransomed be, and raised up from the dead*
> *I gave, I gave My life for thee, what hast thou given for Me?*
> *I gave, I gave My life for thee, what hast thou given for Me?*
>
> *I spent long years for thee, In weariness and woe,*
> *That an eternity, Of joy thou mightest know.*
> *I spent long years for thee: Hast thou spent one for Me?*
> *My Father's house of light, My glory circled throne*
>
> *I left for earthly night, for wanderings sad and lone;*
> *I left, I left it all for thee, hast thou left aught for Me?*
> *I left, I left it all for thee, hast thou left aught for Me?*
> *I suffered much for thee, more than thy tongue can tell,*
>
> *Of bitterest agony, to rescue thee from hell.*
> *I've borne, I've borne it all for thee, what hast thou borne for Me?*
> *I've borne, I've borne it all for thee,*
> *what hast thou borne for Me?*
> *And I have brought to thee, down from My home above,*
>
> *Salvation full and free, My pardon and My love;*
> *I bring, I bring rich gifts to thee, what hast thou brought to Me?*
> *I bring, I bring rich gifts to thee, what hast thou brought to Me?*
> *Great gifts I brought to thee: What hast thou brought to Me?*
>
> *Oh let thy life be given, Thy years for Him be spent,*
> *World-fetters all be riven, And joy with suffering blent.*
> *Bring thou thy worthless all: Follow thy Saviour's call."*

51. HOLY, HOLY, HOLY! LORD GOD ALMIGHTY
(Gw'oli Mutukuvu)
A & M 160   CH 73

"Holy, Holy, Holy" was written by Reginald Heber, an Anglican clergyman, nearly two hundred years ago. He wrote hymns in an attempt to improve the singing in his little congregation at Hodnet, near Birmingham, England.

Most congregations in those days sang the Psalter— but most sang it badly. To inject a bit of spirit in the hymn-singing, Heber introduced his congregation to some of the modern church music of his day, to include John Newton's "Amazing Grace." He also wrote dozens of hymns, the best-known being "Holy, Holy, Holy" prepared for Trinity Sunday, as evidenced by the words, "God in three persons, blessed Trinity," in the first and last verses. But it is this hymn, "Holy, Holy, Holy," that has blessed people all over the world. Translated into many languages and sung in many tongues, it was Rev. Heber's most enduring gift to the church.

At 40 years old, Rev. Heber reluctantly left his beloved England to begin service as Bishop of Calcutta, India. The scope of the job combined with the hot climate and primitive conditions, proved too much for Bishop Heber. He died at the age of 43 after serving only three years in India. His music was Rev. Heber's true legacy that after his death, a hymnal was published that included all of his hymns. Even today, most hymnals include two or three of his hymns.

Later, Reginald Heber's widow found "Holy, Holy, Holy, Lord God Almighty," among her dead husband's papers, words of one of the most powerful and beautiful hymns ever written. But years would pass before the lines took their place in worship services around the world.

In 1861, a publisher rediscovered the words. He asked John Bacchus Dykes to furnish him with a tune. It made sense for him to turn to John who had a natural aptitude for music coupled to his music master that same year. John had been a church organist since he was ten-years-old and was co-founder and president of the Cambridge University Musical Society. John accepted the words and within thirty minutes he wrote the tune "Nicea," after the church council that established the doctrine of the Trinity and also which carried the praise of the Trinity to Christians everywhere.

In 1862, John Dykes was appointed vicar of St. Oswald. This put him in charge of a parish. He was thirty-nine and had already held several lesser church posts. John's people came to love him.

His bishop, however, did not care for John's views. John was "high-church." This meant that he stressed the continuity of the Church of England with the Roman Catholic church from which it had sprung. He believed that church and monarchy had divine rights which were being washed away by modern changes. There was long-lasting disagreement between John and his bishop because of this.

Charles Baring, his bishop, refused to give John any help with his large parish unless he would agree to conduct his services in a more "low-church" style. He had to get rid of colorful collars, stop burning incense and not turn his back on his congregation at times during the service. John wouldn't agree and so he had to handle the whole parish himself, a job which exhausted him.

Nonetheless, in addition to his regular duties, he managed to write over 300 hymn tunes. These included some for our favorite hymns, such as "Jesus, the Very Thought of Thee" and less familiar songs such as "Ten Thousand Times Ten Thousand" and "Lead, Kindly Light."

Worn out with his labors and constant friction with his bishop, John died on this day, January 22, 1876. He was just fifty-three years old. Those who loved and admired him, raised £10,000 to support his widow and children.

Heber's poem sounds to have been inspired by the following scriptures: 1 Samuel 2:2, "There is none holy like God, for there is none besides You, nor is there any rock like our God." ; Revelation 4:8, "And the four living creatures, each having six wings, were full of eyes, around and within. And they do not rest day or night, saying: 'Holy, holy, holy, Lord God Almighty, who was and is and is to come!" Besides, among the most notable and popular a biblical evidence of the Trinity is Christ's prayer for His disciples then and those that would believe on Him later, in John 17:1ff

The issue of the Trinity has for long been perplexing Christians more than possibly any other doctrine since it is so divine and complex to the finite and simplistic minds of the fallen humanity. And all through Christian history, it has been a subject of contention and controversy across the board to the point that up to the present, it still stands out as one doctrine very few preachers would dare talk about in many a congregations, notwithstanding its attacks form the Islamic denominations, as well. But one time I was fortunate to study a publication by one great theologian that I appreciate its beauty and application in our daily Christian living. The book is called "Beyond Life" authored by Gerard Wheeler, he demystified this doctrine by explaining how the God qualities of love and oneness could not have had meaning if God was only in singular, then how would He teach us love if He Himself was in singular. But being in plural (God the Father, the Son and the Holy Ghost) would help to explain the need for unity as the church since even God, despite of being in plural, He (They) act in unity of purpose and everything without ever having any discord or self-interest from the beginning of this world. And oneness doesn't mean singularity but uniqueness, in that there is no other God like Him; keeping in mind the Asian/ Mid-Eastern cultures of having a multiplicity of gods ranging from family gods to village gods to district/ provincial gods, and so on and so forth. God is unique and not like those simplistic gods. He further explains that creating us in His image implies that, as God is in plural, He expects us to: be so hospitable to others and accommodative; to express unity in diversity in the institution of marriage, with dad, mum and children but in harmony and not tyranny; finally harmony and unity in His church despite our differences in resource endowments; heights, levels of education and intelligence, levels of leadership and ministry. This clearly puts Christ's prayer in John 17:1ff, in perspective since He was praying for unity just as Him, God the Father and the Spirit are united and in harmony.

> Holy, Holy, Holy Lord God Almighty
> Early in the morning our song shall rise to Thee;
> Holy, Holy, Holy, Merciful and Mighty!
> God in Three Persons, Blessed Trinity!

> Holy, holy, holy! Angels adore Thee,
> Casting down their bright crowns around the glassy sea;
> Thousands and ten thousands worship low before Thee,
> Who was, and is and ever more shall be.

> Holy, holy, holy! Lord God Almighty!
> All thy works shall praise Thy name in earth and sky and sea;
> Holy, holy, holy! Merciful and mighty!
> God in three persons, blessed Trinity

52. JESUS, KEEP ME NEAR THE CROSS
(Awo Ku Musalaba)
CS 595

Fanny J. Crosby (1820-1915) was the author of over 8,500 gospel songs. Though blind at 6 weeks of age, Crosby began composing texts at age 6. When she was just six-weeks-old, Fanny got an infection that was made worse when a phony doctor poured hot poultice on her inflamed eyes. She became almost completely blind, only able to distinguish day from night. She later became a teacher at the New York School for the Blind, where she was a student. She had an incredible memory and was able to recite whole sections of the Bible, including the Pentateuch, the four Gospels, and all of Proverbs. A friend of several presidents, Crosby became one of the most important advocates for the cause of the blind in the United States.

Her texts were set to the compositions of some of the most prominent gospel song composers of the day including William Bradbury, William Doane and Ira Sankey. She used such pseudonyms and fake names as Victoria Sterling, Sally Smith, and even James Black, and it is said at least 100 pseudonyms were used in her hymn-writing career. She did not always want to be known as the writer of a particular hymn. She married blind musician Alexander Van Alstyne, and the British hymnals identify her as Frances Van Alstyne, her married name.

This hymn was written by Aunt Fanny Crosby. She Co-wrote this hymn with William Doane (1832-1915); who wrote the music first, and then Crosby penned the words we know so well. When in her advanced career Fanny had taken up hymn writing, she turned her poetic skills to hymn writing, and many of her songs focused on the theme of the cross, such as "At the Cross, There's

Room", "Blessed Cross", "Room at the Cross", "Save Me at the Cross", and this one, "Jesus Keep Me Near the Cross". It was composed after Cincinnati businessman William Doane gave her a melody he had written. Fanny, listening to it, felt it said, "Jesus, keep me near the cross," and she promptly wrote the words.

"This hymn is one of many texts by Crosby that combine vivid imagery (blinded in her childhood) and powerful biblical and evangelical metaphors: the Cross, a fountain of healing streams, free grace, the daily walk of faith, God's pursuing love and mercy, Jesus, the Lamb of God, beyond the river of death, and heaven with its golden street", commented by one music expert.

The glory of the Cross, a theme of the refrain, is a common metaphor of Romantic-era hymnody. The Cross, a place where the pain of earth and the joy of heaven come together, is a kind of spiritual altar to which we might draw near for refuge and solace. From it flows a "precious fountain"—an image perhaps borrowed from the 18th-century poet William Cowper and his hymn "There is a fountain filled with blood".

Her words show the familiarity she felt with her Lord: from the 'beams' around her (verse 2), to the cross' 'shadow' over her (verse 3), senses that were sharpened as she pondered the sight she lacked here on earth, but would inherit to see Him in Eternity.

Besides, though an instrument of cruel punishment and torture, the Cross is the source of a "healing stream" (stanza one), and a place where "the bright and morning star sheds its beams" on us (stanza two).

We are invited to meditate upon the Cross in Stanza three, "bring its scenes before me." The "shadow" of the Cross falls on my daily path. This image is suggestive of another Romantic-era poet, Elizabeth C. Clephane, who in 1872 wrote "Beneath the Cross of Jesus".

The famous evangelist Dwight L. Moody was said to have asked Crosby the following question toward the end of her life: "If you could have just one wish granted, what would it be?" Moody expected her to ask for sight. Sensing this she is said to have replied, "If I could have one wish, I'd wish that I might continue blind the rest of my life." Moody was taken back and asked, "How can you say that?" Crosby was said to have responded, "Because, after being blind for all these years, the first face I want to see now is the face of Jesus."

Crosby's poem-turned-hymn can be related to the following scriptures, most of which are Pauline writings, whose core theme is the Cross of Jesus: 1 Corinthians 1:18, "For the preaching of the cross is to them that perish foolishness; but unto us which are saved, it is the power of God." But also, Galatians 6:14, "But God forbid that I should glory, save in the Cross of our Lord Jesus Christ, by whom the world is crucified unto me, and I unto the world". Finally, Philippians 3:18, "For many walk, of whom I have told you often, and now tell you even weeping, that they are the enemies of the cross of Christ".

Had we been living in the day of Christ's crucifixion, I wonder how near we would have been to the cross. The question is, 'would we have gotten close enough to see the anguish on his face, to hear the final words that he spoke, to witness the blood as it poured from his wounds?' Besides, in the real sense, how near are you often to the cross and to the crucified Christ? Our nearness to the cross will be manifest in the life that we live if we are near the cross, it will be reflected in: how we live, what we do, and in our relationships with others. How I pray we could examine our nearness to the Christ of the cross. He died on the cross for our sins so that we might be like Mary Magdalene who encountered a changed life and a better perspective towards discipleship. If we would draw near the cross, we would be able to learn the true value of Christ-like humility, and self-less service. At the cross, one can find the strength to live a committed, dedicated life, and at the cross one can become a caring, compassionate person that the family, the community, the church and Christ would wish you to be. Examine your nearness to the Cross of the crucified Jesus.

Jesus, keep me near the cross,
There a precious fountain,
Free to all, a healing stream
Flows from Calvary's mountain.

Chorus
In the cross, in the cross,
Be my glory ever,
Till my ransomed soul shall find
Rest beyond the river.

Near the cross, a trembling soul,
Love and mercy found me;
There the Bright and Morning Star
Shed His beams around me.

Near the cross! O Lamb of God,
Bring its scenes before me;
Help me walk from day to day
With it's shadows o'er me.

Near the cross! I'll watch and wait,
Hoping, trusting ever,
Till I reach the golden strand,
Just beyond the river.

53. MY JESUS, I LOVE THEE
(Gwe Yesu Omulokozi Nkwagala)
CH 276

William Ralf Featherstone (1846 – 1873) of Montreal, Canada was aged 16 years old when he wrote this simple but philosophical hymn in 1862, soon after his conversion to Christ. William wrote no other known hymn and his brief life ended just before his twenty-seventh birthday.

One would wonder how such an early Teenager could write this thoughtful hymn which showed a deep and established personal relationship with his God. And this can inform us that regardless of one's age, life situation, background, among other variable factors, when someone truly meets Christ, Jesus as Paul did on his way to Damascus, the Holy Ghost bestows a power that surpasses any earthly. May be this power can be likened to the Greek word "dunamis" referring to Christ's life changing power having the force of the dynamite.

The song can be connected to Jesus' strong warning as recorded by Luke, in Luke 14:33, "Any of you who do not give up everything he cannot be My disciple". Besides, this can further be expounded by Paul's epistle to the Philippians on the topic of the priceless value of knowing Christ in Philippians 3:7-8, "I once thought these things were valuable, but now I consider them worthless because of what Christ has done. Yes, everything else is worthless when compared with the infinite value of knowing Christ Jesus my Lord. For His sake, I have discarded everything else, counting it all as garbage, so that I could gain Christ."

Young William had been confronted by his sin and an eternity separated from God. In a life changing moment, he had trusted Jesus to forgive His sin. His experience reminds me of one of the pioneers in the gospel ministry, who lived way before William, called Martin Luther who also one time encountered the desperation that William faced. Luther, it is said, one night after a long day of missionary work, had gone to sleep and he dreamt when he had an encounter with the devil challenging his relationship with the loving Lord. The devil brought a big scroll to Luther's attention, which had all the possible sins and crimes he had committed all through his life, some of which were so dreadful as yours and mine that he never anticipated anyone else either to know or to remind him in life. Then all of a sudden, the devil covered the ending part of this scroll so as to deny Luther the opportunity to establish whether he was forgiven or convicted for eternal death. It is said that he tried to wrestle the devil to uncover the conclusion of it all but Satan progressively denied him access, not until Christ intervened and assured Luther that his sins had been forgiven, and he was then at peace with God. Initially, the devil had tried to discourage him so that he resigns from ministry thinking that his sins were so huge that his ministry would not be approved by God, just the same way the devil tried to make young William guilty so as to resign and only prepare for his judgment. We bless God that He instead encouraged him to stand up as a man of God and claim his repentance by God's grace.

William Featherstone had been transformed into a "new creation," a child of God. Sinfulness had given way to repentance. He experienced the incredible joy of a life purchased by the blood of Jesus. Earlier, Jesus had been just a name, but now Jesus was William's 'Redeemer'. So loved by God, William could write these beautiful words expressing his love for Jesus.

> *My Jesus, I love Thee, I know Thou art mine;*
> *For Thee all the follies of sin I resign.*
> *My gracious Redeemer, my Savior art Thou;*
> *If ever I loved Thee, my Jesus, 'tis now.*
>
> *I love Thee because Thou has first loved me,*
> *And purchased my pardon on Calvary's tree.*
> *I love Thee for wearing the thorns on Thy brow;*
> *If ever I loved Thee, my Jesus, 'tis now.*
>
> *I'll love Thee in life, I will love Thee in death,*
> *And praise Thee as long as Thou lendest me breath;*
> *And say when the death dew lies cold on my brow,*
> *If ever I loved Thee, my Jesus, 'tis now.*
>
> *In mansions of glory and endless delight,*
> *I'll ever adore Thee in heaven so bright;*
> *I'll sing with the glittering crown on my brow;*
> *If ever I loved Thee, my Jesus, 'tis now.*

54. A MIGHTY FORTRESS IS OUR GOD

Martin Luther (1483-1546) was born on November 10, 1483 in Eisleben, Saxony, Germany. He was educated at the University of Erfurt. From a humble home of German peasants, whose father worked as a miner to earn the means for his education, he grew up as a zealous, ardent and devoted man, knowing no fear but the fear of God. Though his father intended him for a lawyer, God purposed him for a builder of His kingdom since he acknowledged no foundation for religious faith but the Holy Scriptures. His parents endowed him with a strong and active mind, fear of the Lord, great force of character, honesty, firmness and straightforwardness. Ellen G. White in The Great Controversy informs that, "At school, where he was sent at an early age, Luther was treated with harshness and even violence. So great was the poverty of his parents that upon going from home to school in another town he was for a time obliged to obtain his food by singing door to door, and he often suffered from hunger." On October 31, 1517, sometimes called the "4th of July of Protestantism," Martin Luther nailed his ninety-five theses to the door of the Cathedral of Wittenberg, Germany. These theses condemned various practices and teachings of the Roman Catholic Church. After several years of stormy disputes with the Pope and other church leaders, Martin Luther was finally excommunicated from the fellowship of the Roman Catholic Church in 1520.

One of the important benefits of the Reformation Movement was the rediscovery of congregational singing. Luther had strong convictions about the use and power of sacred music. He expressed his convictions in this way,

"If any man despises music, as all fanatics do, for him I have no liking; for music is a gift and grace of God, not an invention of men. Thus it drives out the devil and makes people cheerful. Then one forgets all wrath, impurity and other devices." Again, "The Devil, the originator of sorrow, anxieties and restless troubles, flees before the sound of music almost as much as the Word of God."

In another place, "I wish to compose sacred hymns so that the Word of God may dwell among the people also by means of songs." Finally, Luther wrote, "I would allow no man to preach or teach God's people without a proper knowledge of the use and power of sacred song."

The single most powerful hymn of the Protestant Reformation Movement was Luther's "A Mighty Fortress Is Our God," based on Psalm 46. This hymn became the battle cry for the people, a great source of strength and inspiration even for those who were martyred for their convictions. Martin Luther's hymn has often been called the "Battle Hymn of the Reformation" and has been translated into almost every known language. It was perhaps the single most powerful hymn of the Reformation, as it was a great source of strength and inspiration for those who were persecuted and even martyred for their convictions. Martin Luther used Psalm 46 as the inspiration for "A Mighty Fortress Is Our God." Luther's four stanzas interpret this psalm from his own experience during the troubled times of the Reformation. He interpreted the psalm to be not merely expressing God's protection and strength for God's people of Jerusalem, but for God's people of all times. And he understood the battle described in the psalm to be more than an earthly battle but a spiritual battle. So Luther saw in Psalm 46 a great encouragement for him and the Reformers that God would be a strong refuge and strength for them in their current time of trouble, and a battle against not merely fleshly armies but in the realm of spiritual warfare as they defended the Gospel itself.

Luther once said, "We sing this psalm to the praise of God, because God is with us and powerfully and miraculously preserves and defends his church and his word against all fanatical spirits, against the gates of hell, against the implacable hatred of the devil, and against all the assaults of the world, the flesh and sin." It is said of Luther that there were times during the dark and dangerous periods of the Reformation when he was terribly discouraged and depressed. But at such times he would turn to his friend and coworker Philipp Melanchthon and say, "Come, Philipp, let's sing the forty-sixth Psalm." Then they would sing it in Luther's own strong version.... We know it as "A Mighty Fortress Is Our God."

James Montgomery once commented:

"Almost everyone associates Martin Luther with the Book of Romans, particularly Romans 1:17, "The just shall live by faith". We tend to forget that Luther was converted not only by his study of Romans, but also by his study of the psalms. Luther taught the psalms for years and loved them very much, even late in life. His favorite was Psalm 46.

The hymn was based on Psalm 46, a psalm written in response to God's delivering His people from severe calamity and trial. Psalm 46 begins with, "God is our refuge and strength, a very present help in trouble. Therefore we will not fear."

It then describes an event in which the city of Jerusalem was under siege by enemy armies, using pictures of the earth shaking and mountains falling and waters flooding to express how horrible the situation was. Then the psalmist describes how, though the Israelites could do nothing in their own power, God was with His people and He could not be shaken nor moved and He won the victory. The final stanza of the psalm looks ahead to the future when God shall defeat all armies and establish His eternal reign. It presents God as the conqueror who is the one and only victorious and sovereign God. Therefore He tells us: "be still and know that I am God"

Martin Luther's "A Mighty Fortress Is Our God" has often been called the "Battle Hymn of the Reformation" and has been translated into almost every known language. It was perhaps the single most powerful hymn of the Reformation, as it was a great source of strength and inspiration for those who were persecuted and even martyred for their convictions.

Martin Luther used Psalm 46 as the inspiration for "A Mighty Fortress Is Our God." Luther's four stanzas interpret this psalm from his own experience during the troubled times of the Reformation. He interpreted the psalm to be not merely expressing God's protection and strength for God's people of Jerusalem, but for God's people of all times. And he understood the battle described in the psalm to be more than an earthly battle but a spiritual battle. So Luther saw in Psalm 46 a great encouragement for him and the Reformers that God would be a strong refuge and strength for them in their current time of trouble, and a battle against not merely fleshly armies but in the realm of spiritual warfare as they defended the Gospel itself. This prompted Luther to write that, "And though this world with devils filled should threaten to undo us, we will not fear; for God hath willed His truth to triumph through us: The Prince of Darkness grim, we tremble not for him; His rage we can endure, for lo, his doom is sure, one little word shall fell him."

(1) A mighty fortress is our God, a bulwark never failing;
Our helper He, amid the flood of mortal ills prevailing:
For still our ancient foe doth seek to work us woe;
His craft and power are great, and, armed with cruel hate,
On earth is not his equal.

*(2) Did we in our own strength confide, our striving would be losing;
Were not the right Man on our side, the Man of God's own choosing:
Dost ask who that may be? Christ Jesus, it is He;
Lord Sabaoth, His Name, from age to age the same,
And He must win the battle.*

*(3) And though this world, with devils filled, should threaten to undo us,
We will not fear, for God hath willed His truth to triumph through us:
The Prince of Darkness grim, we tremble not for him;
His rage we can endure, for lo, his doom is sure,
One little word shall fell him.*

*(4) That word above all earthly powers, no thanks to them, abideth;
The Spirit and the gifts are ours through Him Who with us sideth:
Let goods and kindred go, this mortal life also;
The body they may kill: God's truth abideth still,
His kingdom is forever.*

55. BRINGING IN THE SHEAVES
(Sowing in the morning)
(Kakano Tusiga)
CH 621

Author: Knowles Shaw (1834-1878)
Composer: George Austin Minor (1845-1904)

Knowles Shaw was born on October 31, 1834, in Butler County, Ohio. When he was only 13 years, Shaw stood at the bedside of his dying father. "Prepare to meet thy God!" said the old man. It is believed that Shaw was the last born of this old father of his and basically the only one available to take care of him. Weighty words from Amos 4:12. And the young man promptly ignored them! Shaw would later turn his God-given talent as a violinist to playing for many community dances, living a careless, fun-filled life.

But five years later, at a rowdy dance party, Knowles Shaw now 18 years, seemed to hear his father's words echoing in his heart. He dropped his violin bow on the spot. Sensing his values were all wrong, he determined never again to use his talent just to amuse the careless crowd. At this stage in his life, Knowles Shaw gave his heart to Christ and prepared for Christian ministry. Records kept at the time suggest that the Lord used him to bring nearly 20,000 people to Christ.

In 1874, he wrote a gospel song called "Bringing in the Sheaves". It is based on Psalm 126:5-6 which says: "Those who sow in tears shall reap in joy. He, who continually goes forth weeping, bearing seed for sowing, shall doubtless come again with rejoicing, bringing his sheaves with him." The song was written for worship in Christian services, and the images of sowing and harvesting in the song are biblical references.

The following letter written by his pastor, elder Kirk Baxter from Dallas, Texas tells of his final day on earth. " Dear Brother: Just one year ago, to-day, Brother Shaw was killed. During his last meeting among the numerous calls to labour at other places, was one from the church at McKinney, which sent a delegation to urge him to visit there, if only for a few days.

Knowles Shaw wrote the music for "Bringing in the Sheaves," in 1874, but was not as well received as would be expected. In 1880 George Austin Minor wrote a new tune for this hymn and it was well received and we still sing it to this tune today.

This Psalm, coupled with the Pauline counsels to the Galatians express a basic principle that can be applied to serving the Lord, "Let us not grow weary while doing good, for in due season we shall reap if we do not lose heart" (Gal. 6:9). These passages remind us there is hard work involved in our service for the Lord, with heavy burdens, and perhaps even tears. But the end result is well worth it. In part, Knowles Shaw's hymn says:

Going forth with weeping, sowing for the Master.
Though the loss sustained our spirit often grieves;
When our weeping's over, He will bid us welcome,
We shall come rejoicing, bringing in the sheaves.
Bringing in the sheaves, bringing in the sheaves,
We shall come rejoicing, bringing in the sheaves.

"Bringing in the Sheaves" is a metaphorical image of harvesting. The Bible makes numerous references to sowing seed, which is understood to be the act of spreading knowledge and truth. Specifically, it refers to telling others about Jesus, who said, "Go ye therefore, and teach all nations baptizing them in the name of the Father, and of the Son, and of the Holy Ghost: Teaching them to observe all things whatsoever I have commanded you: and, lo, I am with you always, even unto the end of the world." (Mathew 28:19-20). With this understanding of the act of sowing (planting seeds), the act of harvesting is then easier to understand. Truth (i.e. knowledge of Jesus) is planted in the hearts and minds of people, which then grows into knowledge, understanding, and belief. The final fruit of that growth is when people believe in Jesus, and choose to follow him. Thus, while the literal image of bringing in sheaves is an image of gathering grain during a harvest, the metaphorical image is one of followers of Jesus presenting to God (Jesus) the new followers that have been brought into his service by their efforts.

The critical part of sowing and reaping is done by God's followers, but the actual work of causing the seed of truth to grow into understanding and belief is the word of God through the Holy Spirit. What an interesting set of metaphors "Sowing in the shadows". This brings to me mental images of a farmer that rises early in the morning and sows in the shadows, and who continues to work into the shadows of the dusk of evening. He has urgency about him and little time. But he can't wait for perfect weather. He can't spread the planting over several months. He must get the seed in the ground. Oh yes, it is hard work and it may bring grief and pain. But there is nothing as rewarding as seeing the abundant fruit of one's labour getting to fruition. It is so encouraging to know that every drop of blood, sweat, and tears has not been in vain but brought a plentiful harvest. We, too, ought to be like this cultivator. We must sow in the shadows, and we must be willing to do the hard work required to get the seed in the ground. The harvest is factual.

(1) Sowing in the morning, sowing seeds of kindness,
Sowing in the noontide and the dewy eve;
Waiting for the harvest, and the time of reaping,
We shall come rejoicing, bringing in the sheaves.

Chorus
Bringing in the sheaves, bringing in the sheaves,
We shall come rejoicing, bringing in the sheaves,
Bringing in the sheaves, bringing in the sheaves,
We shall come rejoicing, bringing in the sheaves,

(2) Sowing in the sunshine, sowing in the shadows,
Fearing neither clouds nor winter's chilling breeze;
By and by the harvest and the labour ended,
We shall come rejoicing, bringing in the sheaves.

(3) Going forth with weeping, sowing for the Master,
Though the loss sustained our spirit often grieves;
When our weeping's over, He will bid us welcome,
We shall come rejoicing, bringing in the sheaves.

56. JUST AS I AM
(Mukama Nze Nina Ebibi)
A & M 349   CH 222

Charlotte Elliott (1789-1871) was a poet and a popular musician. Charlotte's story of protracted struggle against the oppressive power of sin provides a helpful lesson to Christians and non-Christians alike. At an early age, Charlotte began to be aware of her sinful nature and of her impotence to resist sin's enticements. Growing up, Charlotte felt herself increasingly unworthy of God's grace and incapable of facing a perfect and righteous God.

It is said that one day, an elderly man approached her at a dinner party and asked if she was a Christian. She considered him rude and unkind, and that his question was inappropriate. After the man walked away, Charlotte could not get his question out of her mind so she went to find the man, and to ask how to become a Christian but she didn't find him anywhere.

Charlotte once lamented, "My Heavenly Father knows, and He alone, what it is, day after day, and hour after hour, to fight against bodily feelings of almost overpowering weakness and languor and exhaustion, to resolve, as He enables me to do, not to yield to the sluggishness, the depression, the irritability, such as a body causes me to long to indulge, but to rise every morning determined on taking this for my motto, 'If any man will come after me, let him deny himself, take up his cross daily, and follow me." She visited many churches and solicited the help of many pastors, all of whom counselled her simply to pray more, to study the Bible more, to perform more noble deeds, and to resolve to do better. However, all the advice she received was unavailing. For seven or eight more years, Charlotte continued struggling in vain against sin, all the while caught up in self-condemnation. She experienced at length the despondency of the human condition described in Romans 7:18: "I know that in me...nothing good dwells; for to will [the good] is present with me, but to work out the good is not."

After some time, Charlotte Elliott met an eminent preacher named Dr. Caesar Malan. This encounter would prove to be a great turning point in Charlotte's life. She asked him, as she had asked many others, how she might be saved. Sensing the enormous burden weighing upon her conscience, Malan responded compassionately, "Go to God just as you are." Charlotte asked him incredulously, "Do I not have to do better, make more progress, and improve more before I believe in the Lord Jesus?" Malan simply repeated this simple, priceless phrase: "You must come to Him just as you are." These few liberating words of fellowship had a deep and ineffaceable effect on Charlotte Elliott and would later inspire the composition of her best-known hymn, "Just as I Am." In 1835, about twelve years after her conversion, her brother was raising funds for a school for the daughters of clergymen--St. Mary's Hall. Unable to help with the project, Charlotte felt useless. Perhaps God had even rejected her! She fell into deep doubt. As she pondered her situation, she remembered the words of Cesar Malan and decided to write a song for others who were in her situation. The words she wrote became one of the greatest soul-winning songs in the history of hymns.

This hymn was made especially popular in the 20th century as the 'official' altar call song of the Billy Graham Crusades. Many souls have found Jesus as Saviour in response to the simple beauty of this song. Over the remainder of her life Charlotte wrote 150 hymns.

This hymn story is connected to Romans 7:18-19, "And I know that nothing good lives in me, that is, in my sinful nature. I want to do what is right, but I can't. I want to do what is good, but I don't. I don't what to do what is wrong, but I do it anyway." The 'power within' is the sin nature deep within us. This is our vulnerability to sin; it refers to everything within us that is more loyal to our old way/ lifestyle of selfish living than to God.

There is great tension in daily Christian experience. The conflict is that we agree with God's commands but can't do them. As a result, we are painfully aware of our sin, and this inward struggle with sin was real for the Apostle as well as for Charlotte as it is for us to the present. From Paul we learn what to do about it. Whenever he felt overwhelmed by the spiritual battle, he would return to the beginnings of his spiritual life, remembering how he had been freed from sin by Jesus Christ. When we feel confused and overwhelmed by sin's appeal, let us claim the freedom Christ gave us because His power can lift us to victory.

Just as I am, without one plea,
But that Thy Blood was shed for me,
And that Thou bidst me come to Thee,
   O Lamb of God, I come, I come!

Just as I am, and waiting not
To rid my soul of one dark blot,
To thee, whose Blood can
cleanse each spot,
   O Lamb of God, I come, I come!

Just as I am, though tossed about
With many a conflict, many a doubt,
Fightings and fears within, without,
   O Lamb of God, I come, I come!

Just as I am, poor, wretched, blind;
Sight, riches, healing of the mind,
Yea, all I need, in Thee to find,
   O Lamb of God, I come, I come!

Just as I am; Thou wilt receive,
Wilt welcome, pardon, cleanse, relieve,
Because Thy promise I believe;
   O Lamb of God, I come, I come!

Just as I am, Thy Love unkown
Has broken every barrier down;
Now to be Thine, yea, Thine alone,
   O Lamb of God, I come, I come.

57. LORD, I'M COMING HOME
(Nakyama Okuva Ku Yesu)
CS 560

William J. Kirkpatrick (1838-1921) wrote the music to many of our favourite hymns. Born in Duncannon, Pennsylvania in 1838, William learned to play musical instruments at an early age and received formal training. He was not only a marvellous lyricist, but his musical settings for poems written by others have afforded us such favourites as: "We Have Heard the Joyful Sound," "'Tis Sweet to Trust in Jesus," "Redeemed, How I Love to Proclaim It," and "He Hideth My Soul."He published his first hymn collection at age 21, but although he issued around fifty books of music in his life, he often found it necessary to support himself with carpentry or furniture making, although he devoted every spare moment to music, playing for churches and writing hymn tunes. Even his service with the Union armies in the Civil War was as a musician, fifth major to the 91st Regiment P. V. Not until after the death of his first wife in 1878 was he able to devote himself full time to music.

William J. Kirkpatrick was a Methodist choir director and organist, and he especially loved the Methodist camp meetings. He wrote both the words and the music to the song "Lord, I'm Coming Home". The story behind it shows him as a soul-winner. During one such meeting, at which he directed the music, he became quite burdened because the invited soloist would sing and then immediately leave, without hearing the sermon. The hired vocalist had a magnificent voice, able to put tremendous expression into the music he sang.

After a couple of days of this, Kirkpatrick prayed fervently that God would somehow reach this young man with the gospel of

Christ. He feared that the singer had never really known Christ as Saviour.

As a result, God gave a beautiful song to William Kirkpatrick; he wrote the words down and set them to a haunting tune, which he asked the soloist to sing during an evening service of the meetings. He did so, and he was so convicted in his heart as he sang the words that he decided to stay and hear the sermon. Following the sermon, the singer knelt at the altar and was gloriously converted. The song became a popular invitation hymn in evangelical services, winning many others beside the man it was written for.

Nineteen years later, at age eighty-three, Kirkpatrick was sitting up late, working on a music composition. His wife awakened and noticed that the lights were still on in his study. After calling out to him and hearing no response, she went quickly to his study and found him slumped over his last musical offering.

This hymn is related to Christ's kind appeal in Mathew 11:28-30, "Then Jesus said, 'Come to me all of you who are weary and heavy burdens and I will give you rest. Take my yoke upon you. Let me teach you, because I am humble and gentle at heart, and you will find rest for your souls. For my yoke is easy to bear, and the burden I give you is light." A yoke is a heavy wooden harness that fits over the shoulders of oxen. It is attached to the piece of equipment the oxen are to pull. Someone may be carrying heavy burdens of: sin, excessive demands of religion, oppression and persecution, and weariness in the search for God. Christ frees people from all these burdens. The rest that Jesus promises is love, healing, and peace with God, not the end of all labor. A relationship with God changes meaningless wearisome toil into spiritual productivity and purpose. Jesus doesn't offer a life of luxurious ease: the yoke is still an oxen's tool for working hard. But it is a shared yoke, with weight falling on bigger shoulders than yours.

As we cry out to God to lead us home again, my prayer is that we desist from behaving like a certain lady who was so overloaded with: a luggage on the head, a baby on the back, a huge bag in her hands. She was travelling and suddenly she saw a vehicle which she asked for a lift to her destination. The driver was moved by compassion over a lady who was so loaded, and so he took her into the car, and then continued their journey. Later, she realized through the driver's mirror that the lady didn't unload herself despite having been given a lift: she continued carrying the luggage on the head; baby on the back and the big bag in her hands. Rather furious, the driver ordered the lady to relieve of herself all the load she had but all his initiative was in vain, not until he had to leave the troubled lady in peace so that she could continue carrying her load as she chose to do but frustrating the driver's intentions of relieving her of the burdens of this world at least during their travel in the vehicle. In a like manner, many Christians crave to come home but they remain so glued to their earthly cares, burdens and sins that have always worn their lives out, hence rendering Christ's redemptive initiatives futile and with no avail.

(1) I've wandered far away from God,
Now I'm coming home;
The paths of sin too long I've trod,
Lord, I'm coming home.

Chorus

Coming home, coming home,
Nevermore to roam,
Open wide Thine arms of love,
Lord, I'm coming home.

(2) I've wasted many precious years,
Now I'm coming home;
I now repent with bitter tears,
Lord, I'm coming home.

(3) I'm tired of sin and straying, Lord,
Now I'm coming home;
I'll trust Thy love, believe Thy Word,
Lord, I'm coming home.

(4) My soul is sick, my heart is sore,
Now I'm coming home;
My strength renew, my hope restore,
Lord, I'm coming home.

58. CHIEF OF SINNERS THOUGH I BE
(Yewaayo Ku Lwange)
CH 238

This hymn was authored by William McComb (1793- 1873) and later it was set to music by Richard Redhead (1820- 1901).The hymn uses Paul's confession: "Christ came to save sinners, of whom I am the chief!" We live in a world that dislikes acknowledging one's wrongs because it is viewed as weakness and culpability that can erode away one's reputation. The contemporary perverse world warns us of the great harm we do to our children if we ever rebuke them or tell them their choices are wrong, which is in itself missing the crucial point. This hymn can be used to impress on all of us that we do have sins – great sins, in fact – that we need to confess and help our children learn to do so, and teach them through these words that God has an unimaginable love that washes those sins away and makes us His dearly loved children.

This hymn was inspired by Paul's counsels to both Jews and gentiles in the Diaspora in Romans 5:8- 11, "But God demonstrates His own love toward us, in that while we were still sinners, Christ died for us. Much more then, having now been justified by His blood, we shall be saved from wrath through Him. For if when we were still enemies we were reconciled to God through the death of His Son, much more, having been reconciled, we shall be saved by His life. And not only that, but we also rejoice in God through our Lord Jesus Christ, through whom we have now received the reconciliation."

This hymn reminds me of a story of a certain man who had enjoyed popularity in his life: a good career, wealthy, and a happy family. As he grew old, he was attacked by a strange disease that didn't only destabilize his life but procured him amnesia (completely lost his memory) to the point that he wasn't only rendered incapable of remembering and recognizing his wife and children but any other details including his name and who he actually was. This was so devastating to the family at large since he was so helpless and such an invalid. On the contrary, at the peak of this desperate state-of-affairs, this old man had the courage to, "I may fail to recall any important details of my life: wife, children, career, relatives, likes & dislikes, including my own name; but there are two most crucial facts that this amnesia (loss of memory) can't steal away from my memory. The first one being that I'm the chief of sinners the world has ever had, and the second one & perhaps the most significant, being that Christ Jesus is the greatest Redeemer/ Saviour the world has ever had in its history. And given His redemptive power, he cleanses away my wickedness and wretchedness so as to give me the hope and joy which can keep me moving in this world."

What a powerful sermon!! If only we could all appreciate and possibly acknowledge our sinfulness (chief of sinners), we shall no more be judgmental and pin point our errant brethrens, but we shall also learn to accommodate and embrace those who have sinned and may have wronged us. We shall have the courage to do what Christ did to the Pharisees who were inclined to stoning the adulterous Mary before she had fully yielded her life to Christ; through love, protect those who have been written off because of their sinfulness. We shall learn to look for that small/ minute good thing in those who have been branded social outcasts, excommunicated, dis-fellowshipped, and possibly condemned to the devil. It is so disheartening that we are so fast at condemning even the slightest of mistakes and turn out to be so accusatory which is actually so characteristic of people who have incidentally not developed a concrete and personal relationship with Christ. This prompted William McComb to declare this counsel in the 3rd Stanza, "Only Jesus can impart Balm to heal the wounded heart, Peace that flows from sin forgiving, Joy that lifts the soul to heaven; Faith and hope to walk with God In the way that Enoch trod."

May we take this hymn as not only a devotional but an inspirational through this sinful world where we dwell with fellow sinners!!

> Chief of sinners though I be, Jesus shed His blood for me;
> Died that I might live on high, Lived that I might never die.
> As the branch is to the vine, I am His and He is mine.
>
> O the height of Jesus' love! Higher than the heaven above,
> Deeper than the deepest sea, Lasting as eternity;
> Love that found me wondrous thought!
> Found me when I sought Him not!
>
> Chief of sinners though I be, Christ is all in all to me;
> All my wants to Him are known, All my sorrows are His own;
> Safe with Him from earthly strife, He sustains the hidden life.

59. THE MESSIAH

George Frideric Handel (1685 – 1759) was the author of this magnificent and "eternal" hymn. The choice of the expression eternal is implied in the glory of the One (King of kings) the hymn eulogizes but neither the author nor the song per se. Handel was not only a great musician but also a wealthy personality and equally popular during his time. He is believed to have authored a big number of hymns and perhaps a couple of secular songs in the early 18th Century.

One gloomy day, he became so ill that he progressively lost his health, to the point that his right side was completely paralyzed. In the process, all his wealth and above all his money was gone; and his creditors seized his estates (property) but these were good enough to cover for the claims/ debts he had with his creditors. This saw him being threatened to be imprisoned as a way of, may be, recovering their money; this only compounded Handel's pathetic situation, and sent him into more desperation. He was so disheartened by this tragic experience for a certain period, but, thanks to God, his faith was later rekindled and then it prevailed.

One bitterly cold winter of 1741, Handel received a package in his lodging. It contained a text made up of Scripture from his friend Charles Jennens: "Comfort ye, comfort ye, My people, says your God...Behold! A virgin shall conceive and bear a Son, and shall call His name Emmanuel; God with us...and His name shall be called Wonderful, Counsellor, The Mighty God..."

Excitedly, he read on, "He was despised and rejected of men; a man of sorrows...I know that my Redeemer lives, and that He shall stand at the latter day upon the earth...King of Kings, and Lord of Lords, Hallelujah!"

Handel rushed to the piano with pencil in hand and began to write the music to the eternal song "The Messiah", which is the bigger hymn, and where "The Hallelujah Choir" is derived. For two weeks, he laboured incessantly, meeting no one and refused food and sleep. At last he finished the great oratorio, and tears were streaming down his face, as he said: "I did think I did see all Heaven before me, and the great God Himself."

The composition was first heard in Dublin where it was an overwhelming success. On the 23rd March 1743, "The Messiah" was performed for the first time in London, England, and the king of England, George 1, had graced the occasion. The king was so moved by the singing of "The Hallelujah Chorus" that he spontaneously stood to his feet and remained standing until the end of Handel's masterpiece (and it is common knowledge that when the king stands up, everybody stands up). Ever since that day, it has been customary for the audience to stand whenever the "Hallelujah Chorus" is sung. (Though some critics say that the king stood up simply desiring to change his position due to the physical relief needed for a two-hour performance of the traditional song "The Messiah").

The hymn can be connected to John's writings in Revelation 17:14, "These will make war with the Lamb, and the Lamb will overcome them, for He is Lord of lords, and King of kings; and those who are with Him are called, chosen, and faithful." But also Revelation 19:16, "And He has on His robe and on His thigh a name written: KING OF KINGS and LORD OF LORDS".

One day, this song was sung and when it rose to its awesome heights, "King of kings, and Lord of lords,..." one pious old Christian man could hardly contain himself. As tears streamed from his eyes, he whispered to his friend: "That was my Saviour they were singing about." And this reminds me of Martin Luther's strong statement, "The heart of religion is in its personal pronoun." This signifies that Christians, our youths, our fathers, mothers, husbands, wives, children to fully yield to God; they should take Him as their (personal) Saviour not as a collective/ corporate/ group Saviour. This is how Martin Luther's counsel can impact my life if I relate directly and personally with my God, then I don't need my parents, my wife, pastor, my elder, my priest, my reverend, my government to be with me so as to take a rational and godly decision since my Lord will be there to guide and encourage me to have a Christ-like attitude and behaviour regardless of how painful and costly it would appear to me. I'll require the presence of my wife and children so as not to yield to seduction from promiscuous women and may be my bodily/ sinful desire of either fornication or adultery. It will not require either higher authorities or the government system to be present as I make decision on whether to swindle or misappropriate resources that are not meant to be mine. The church doesn't need to put up sanctions and stringent systems for me to be able to express my faithfulness in tithing and offerings as long as I acknowledge Christ to be my own Saviour.

How I pray that this hymn revives us to be able to rediscover ourselves as Christians and to walk a faithful journey as Christian men and women!!

Hallelujah! Hallelujah! Hallelujah! Hallelujah! Hallelujah!
For the Lord God Omnipotent reigns.
Hallelujah! Hallelujah! Hallelujah! Hallelujah!

For the Lord God Omnipotent reigns.
Hallelujah! Hallelujah! Hallelujah! Hallelujah!
Hallelujah! Hallelujah! Hallelujah!

*The kingdom of this world is become the kingdom of our Lord,
And of His Christ, and of His Christ;
And He shall reign forever and ever, forever
and ever, forever and ever,*

*King of kings, and Lord of lords, King of kings and Lord of lords,
And Lord of lords, and He shall reign, and
He shall reign forever and ever,
King of kings, forever and ever, and Lord
of lords, Hallelujah! Hallelujah!*

*And He shall reign forever and ever, King
of kings! And Lord of lords!
And He shall reign forever and ever, King
of kings! And Lord of lords!
Hallelujah! Hallelujah! Hallelujah! Hallelujah! Hallelujah!*

60. BENEATH THE CROSS OF JESUS
(Wansi w'Omusalaba We Nyimirira Nze)
CH 280

Elizabeth Clephane was born in Edinburgh, Scotland in 1830 and lived most of her life in the village of Melrose. Her father was the county sheriff but both parents died while she was still young. Clephane was a woman acquainted with grief; her health was so fragile, but never let that stop her. Nevertheless, she was one of those cheerful people who brighten everyone who could come her way. Perhaps because she focused on what she could do for others rather than sitting and feeling sorry for herself, and possibly wishing other to go the agony she was facing. . Her friends called her "Sunbeam", a nick-name that may have inspired the lines in this hymn that say:

> "I ask no other sunshine than
> The sunshine of His face."

Clephane loved poetry and wrote several hymns, among others which could be familiar is "The Ninety and Nine," a hymn inspired by Jesus' parable about a shepherd who had a hundred sheep, but left the ninety-nine to search for the one that was lost – a parable about God's love (Matthew 18:12-14).

In her hymn, "Beneath the Cross of Jesus," Elizabeth alluded to a passage in Isaiah that speaks of "the shade of a great rock in a weary land" (Isaiah 32:1-2). In her hymn, she speaks of:

> "The shadow of a mighty rock
> Within a weary land,
> A home within the wilderness,
> A rest upon the way,
> From the burning of the noontide heat
> And the burden of the day."

Perhaps one reason that this hymn has enjoyed such popularity is that we know what it means to live in a weary land. We feel the need of a mighty rock to shelter us from the heat. Elizabeth says that, for her, Jesus' cross is that resting place. For her, Jesus' cross is her home within the wilderness, her rest upon the way.

There is a fourth stanza of this hymn that is hardly found in many modern hymn books. It brings to reality the big contrast between the character and love of the Christ on the cross and our fallen and desperate nature of sinful. From one version of hymns, it can loosely be translated as: There are two amazing facts that I can't help but to proclaim; My sins are so enormous, and your love is greatly enormous; Your cross delights me above any other thing on earth; I'm letting the world go since I have seen the glory on the cross.

This hymn reminds me of a story of a certain man who had enjoyed popularity in his life: a good career, wealthy, and a happy family. As he grew old, he was attacked by a strange disease that didn't only destabilize his life but procured him amnesia (completely lost his memory) to the point that he wasn't only rendered incapable of remembering and recognizing his wife and children but any other details including his name and who he actually was. This was so devastating to the family at large since he was so helpless and such an invalid. On the contrary, at the peak of this desperate state-of-affairs, this old man had the courage to, "I may fail to recall any important details of my life: wife, children, career, relatives, likes & dislikes, including my own name; but there are two most crucial facts that this amnesia (loss of memory) can't steal away from my memory. The first one being that I'm the chief of sinners the world has ever had, and the second one & perhaps the most significant, being that Christ Jesus is the greatest Redeemer/ Saviour the world has ever had in its history. And given His redemptive power, he cleanses away my wickedness and wretchedness so as to give me the hope and joy which can keep me moving in this world."

The critical question is how valuable do we take the cross of Jesus? How precious do we value the Christ of the cross?

This further reminds me of a story about one man who, due to biting poverty, was advised by a friend to be taken to a foreign land, where there are mineral resources, in particular, gold so as to go, work and better his livelihood since life was progressively becoming a nightmare to this guy by the day. Upon his consent, they embarked on the journey for some days, and on arrival this poor man was shown an area that supposedly had gold in the underground, which required his effort in excavation, and also agreed that as compensation, the friend he brought would take half of the gold that this poor old guy would acquire. He excavated for a couple of days, and got some glittering substance that overjoyed him but on showing his friend (boss), he told him to work a lot more since what he had discovered was not gold. So discouraged, he went ahead to unearth for a lot more days, and he arrived at a very gold-like metal, and with a lot of happiness he took it to the boss, who only felt sorry for him and admonished to remember where he came from so as to be motivated to focus on the job more. This happened for more two times not until finally he landed on the real gold, at this stage he had become so exhausted, in bad shape and rather gripped by desperation. Filled with awe, he went ahead to meet his boss who commended him for the good job and later did according to the contract. This poor-guy-millionaire begun his journey back home, he'd put his treasure in a dirty sack as he boarded a ferry and he was actually in a very horrible shape due to tiring work. He realized that other passengers had not recognized how rich he was, so he removed his gold and all eyes now turned to him despite his bad look. He later turned dramatic as he begun to make fun of other passengers: on lifting the gold up, all faces would go up; down, all heads would go down; throwing it up, all would jump with the gold. And so he continued with the drama, as everyone stood in admiration and wishful thinking; not until one time he threw it up and only to escape his hands and drown deep in the sea. All would had admired him turned into his tormenters, as they jeered, cursed, condemned and despised him; and the best he could was to agonize as he could remember the poverty he'd left, the long periods of work for this gold, and possibly the blissful life he was soon to enjoy. This story informs us about the way we also take the treasure in Jesus of the cross, and how many will end up losing everything due to failure to safeguard the value in Jesus. How I pray that as we contemplate on the hymn "Beneath the Cross of Jesus", our souls might be lifted up to appreciate the value of Christ's cross!!!!

REFERENCES

Billy Graham (1967) Crusader Hymns & Hymn Stories. Billy Graham Evangelistic Association. Chicago, Illinois

Brown, Theron & Butterworth, Hezekiah (1905) The Story of the Hymns & Tunes. New York

Codner, Elizabeth (1880) Among the Brambles, and Other Lessons of Life. London. Nisbert-James

Ellen, G. White (2012) The Great Hope. East-Central Africa Division Publishing Association

Ellen, G. White (1954) Child Guidance. Ellen G. White Publications

Hatfield F Edwin (1884) The Poets of the Church. New York – Anson Randolph

Hauessler, Armin (1952) The Story of our Hymns: the Handbook to the Hymnal of Evangelical & Reformed Church. Eden Publishing

Henry, Gariepy (1970) Songs in the Night. Eerdman's Publishing

Kenneth W Osbeck (1990) Amazing Grace: 366 Inspiring Hymn Stories for Daily Devotions. Kregel Publications, Grand Rapids

Kenneth W Osbeck (1982) 101 Hymn Stories. Kregel Publications, Grand Rapids

Louis F Benson (1915) The English Hymn: Its Development & Use in Worship. Richmond

Mugerwa, Paul (2015) Foundations of Risk Management and the Insurance Device: An Overview of Corporate and Personal Risks, Policies and Systems; & Insurance device in Frontier Economies (Unpublished)

Mugerwa, Paul (2015) ESG (environmental, social & governance) Issues and the Strategic Asset Allocation of Institutional Investors: A case of Uganda, a Non-Signatory Country to UN PRI (To be Published by United Nations' Principles of Responsible Investing)

Smith E Munson (1885) Woman in Sacred Song. Boston – Lothrop

Richard N Donovan (2014) Stories Behind Great Christian Hymns.

Roger Kamien (1998) Music: An Appreciation – Third Brief Edition. The McGraw-Hill Companies

Singo, Andrew (2006) In God's Time: Being the Best You can be. The Stanborough Press Ltd

The Guinness Book of World Records 2015

Wells R Amos (1945) A Treasure of Hymns: Brief Biographies of 120 Leading Hymn-writers & Their Best Hymns. Boston W.A Wilde

Wheeler, Gerald (1998) Beyond Life: What God Says About Life, Death, and Immortality. Review and Herald Publishing Association.

www.resort.com/~prime 8// Orwell/whywrite.html

www.reformedanswers.org/montgomery

www.hymnary.org/person/Heber_Reginald

www.dsgraves.com/christian-History

www.christianity.com/hymn Stories

www.spaffordcentre.org/history

www.challies.com/articles/hymn-stories-my-jesus-i-love-thee

www.ingramcontent.com/pod-product-compliance
Lightning Source LLC
Chambersburg PA
CBHW050905300426
44111CB00010B/1389